PERIPHERAL
VISIONS

Also By Phyllis Theroux

CALIFORNIA AND OTHER STATES OF GRACE

PERIPHERAL

VISIONS

Phyllis Theroux

WILLIAM MORROW AND COMPANY, INC.

New York   1982

All of the essays in this collection were previously published in *The New York Times* except "Fear of Landing" and "The Bully," previously published in *The Washington Post Magazine* (the latter under a different title); "Some Easter," an original piece; "On Hating Piano Lessons," previously published in *Parents Magazine*; and "The Price of Love," previously published in *Mademoiselle*.

Library of Congress Cataloging in Publication Data

Theroux, Phyllis.
   Peripheral visions.

   I. Title.
AC8.T4515   1982   081   81-11101
ISBN 0-688-00788-0   AACR2

Printed in the United States of America

First Edition

1 2 3 4 5 6 7 8 9 10

BOOK DESIGN BY MICHAEL MAUCERI

For Christian, Eliza, and Justin

When my brother was five years old, he found an old skeleton key in the garden. He picked it up and toddled over to my father.

"What's this?" he asked, handing the key to my father.

My father leaned back on his heels, took the key from my brother's hand, and smiled with recognition. "Why, this is the key to the situation."

"What's a situation?" asked my brother, taking the key back.

"It's around here somewhere," said my father, "you go and look for it."

And my brother did. But by the time he found the situation, he had lost the key.

Contents

Introduction

When I was ten years old, I stepped into my first sailboat alone. It was a small, one-passenger dinghy, hardly more than a walnut shell with a board nailed across the middle, and as I grasped the tiller and observed how the breeze filled up the sail, drawing the boat gently away from the dock, I marveled at how easy a thing sailing was. I was wrong.

After the boat had gotten a fair distance away from the dock, the wind picked up force, the mast snapped to attention, and the sail was suddenly full of dangerous ideas that set the boat racing well ahead of my ability to control it. I tugged at the sheet rope, which, in my inexperience, I thought would rein the boat back, like a horse. The boat responded by bucking sideways at a frightening angle to the water, an angle I tried to correct by tugging on the sheet rope even harder and leaning away from the gunwale, which was about to take on the lagoon. Nothing worked. We were, I saw, going to capsize. In desperation I tossed the sheet rope away, dove for the bottom of the boat, and waited for the end.

That decision, born of total inexpertise, turned out to be the correct nautical judgment. The boat, now free of restraints, instantly swung into the wind, righted itself, and when I looked up from my cowardly crouch, the sail was flapping idly against the mast, waiting for a real captain to sail the boat home.

That afternoon I learned the first rule of sailing, respect for the wind. I also gained a rudimentary understanding of how power of any kind operates. The trick in sailing (as in writing or living) lies in knowing what is possible under the circumstances. Circumstances are the raw material for any voyage, and as I tacked clumsily back and forth across the invisible line of my vision toward the dock, I learned that somewhere between absolute control of, and absolute surrender to, circumstances lies the way home.

I did not, as the extended use of this sailing metaphor might imply, go on to accomplish great things on the water. But an essay could be defined as a short trip in a small boat bearing one or two ideas that the writer hopes to "get across." The essays in this book are powered by the circumstances of my life—past as well as present—and while it may appear that the author's whole life is more or less contained in these pages, that is not the case. Most writers try, as the expression goes, to "put their heart" into their work, but they take it back, leaving an imprint whose contours hopefully evoke a cry of recognition from the reader as being similar to his own.

I have also discovered a paradox, which I pass on for what it's worth. Ideas, like children (who surface regularly on these pages at various ages), do not come from nowhere. But they seem to have their own gestation period, collecting themselves up in bits and pieces, forcing one to wait for them. That is the difficult part of writing, the waiting, since by nature I am impatient and time—when its contents confuse or burden me—can seem endless and without significance, a dimension it is difficult to be without.

But whenever I have taken the questions that burn me and set them aside to focus upon something else, I have oftentimes found what I was looking for in a place where I would not have had the imagination to look. Gardening, sorting laundry, peering into the bowels of my piano to see why B flat wasn't working: time and time again, ideas I was struggling with surrendered once I had released my death grip upon wanting to control them. "Burning questions" cooled down after I had consigned them to the corner of my eye.

The trick which takes a lifetime to master is to honor the corner of one's eye without losing sight of what lies directly in front of you. Most writers, for instance, have a vision of something they see in the distance. Using the outward circumstances of their lives, they tack back and forth across that line of vision in order to get a closer look. Often, upon drawing nearer, what I saw from a distance was usually far more interesting than originally perceived, at least more interesting to me. Of course, lines of vision differ. Whether these lines hold up in your mind remains to be seen or not—by you.

I.

Fear of Landing

The convent was an Elysian Fields of sorts, although for every pink-cheeked girl swinging a hockey stick across the grass, there was an old scar-face off campus undoubtedly moving heaven and earth to meet the tuition payments. But we didn't know this. The school threw up a complex of arches, walkways, and corridors which shielded us from gratuitous evil.

In the fall, eucalyptus pods rattled down the roof tiles onto the paths. Spring sent hawthorn blossoms sifting across the inner courtyard, and by June wisteria choked the chicken-wire canopy of the summer-house with purple flowers. It being California, there was no winter worth mentioning.

On Sundays everyone went out with their families. Trooping out between the cool vanilla robes of the sisters at the door, two hundred girls were handed over to the world for an afternoon. The world came to call with lined faces and the smell of cigarettes. We filled up the waiting cars, the taste of doughnuts lingering on our lips, and with the exception of a few malcontents whose spirits were sufficiently developed (or deformed) to complain, we were content. The nuns threw a long, benevolent shadow over us, tallying up the weekly merits and demerits of our lives, like so many accountants bent upon balancing us to perfection. We adored them.

In 1957 the sisters were so totally bound up from head to foot as to be objects of prurient interest. The slight mist of sweat across Sister Carole's brow as she dissected a frog in biology lab was as interesting to me as the still thumping heart she lifted with tweezers from the frog's chest cavity. The fact that Sister Alice had hairs growing from her chin, or that Sister Gregory blushed when embarrassed—these were the thrilling, telltale clues which pointed to humanity beneath their scapulars. Wise virgins holding their lamps so that the foolish ones could better understand the truth, we existed together in sunny dependence, and in those tuition-backed days of simplicity, life was mapped out chronologically into Sacraments you had, or hadn't, received and States of Life you were, or weren't, good enough for.

"Chastity," said Sister Gregory, coloring at the word, "is to be maintained before the Sacrament of Marriage"—so far I followed her—"and *within* the Sacrament of Marriage, too." What? But it seemed a small point. Our lives were breathtakingly pure by any standard, and it was assumed that going to college would prove whether the seed had fallen upon good soil or bad.

College. Marriage. Offspring. Such a slow, unremarkable falling from grace. Loud with children, layered with responsibilities, my judgments threatened like bread crumbs on the trail, there came a time. From this window and that one, upstairs and down, I pulled the curtains from the rods until one day my "house" was a series of glass panes—cold and unwashed, but for all that offering a view. Winter. But I no longer referred to the liturgical calendar. This one was in my bones and cheerfulness no longer carried the day. My nuns were 3,000 miles away, Fulton Sheen was an old man reading yellowed press clippings, and Gloria Steinem was a bad dream smiling beatifically through aviator goggles. My only consolation during this solstice was that God allowed me to think I was going through a unique experience.

Last Christmas my two best friends from the convent announced, via Christmas cards, that they had gotten divorced. The news was unexpected, disturbing, and not a little threatening. They were neither flighty nor avant-garde. Indeed, they were the kind of girls who had offhandedly walked away with prizes that I used to struggle to gain at any price. It shouldn't have happened, not to them.

With odd synchronicity my old English teacher, Sister Rose, wrote several weeks later to say that she was coming to town for a conference. In the seventeen-year interim she had risen to become president of the Catholic college which adjoined the convent campus. Would I like to get together? I most certainly would. It had been a long time and I could embrace her as the valued nun and tutor she was. Then, too, she might know about the divorces.

The lobby of the Hilton was light years away from our old stamping grounds. Waiting for Sister Rose, I noticed that the magazine rack was packed tight with Erica Jong's *Fear of Flying*. That's the kind of book a Catholic girl could not easily write. Too many benedictions with the light pouring through a raised monstrance conspired against it.

Here was Sister Rose, dashing across the carpet, a few additional lines, a slightly thickened waistline, and a shortened, all-around habit which seemed to ground her in a new way. Yet, except for these few corrections in the margin, Sister Rose was remarkably the same. We found a table in the Hilton Hotel coffeeshop and began at the end.

The two divorces . . .

Yes, she knew about them. A sigh. Wasn't it too bad? No, she did not have any details, but "perhaps," she said cautiously, "like a lot of men, their husbands got to a certain age and the responsibilities became too much for them."

Odd, I thought, that she had skipped over their wives. I scanned her face for indications of information in reserve and concluded that she had given me the bulk of her research.

They had been such special girls, I told her, so warm and wonderful. I confessed to having envied them both. Sister Rose nodded.

"You know," she said, "when I think about the three girls I most envied in high school, they have all had hard lives. One of them is dead, another is divorced and never remarried, and the third had a husband who died at home under what some people considered rather suspicious circumstances."

"Suicide?" I prodded.

"No," she replied.

There was no need to comment that Sister Rose had risen to the top, yet there was no smugness in her voice. Like a tennis player peripherally aware of matches on other courts, she heard the balls thwack but was in no position to analyze their strokes. Her own game was sufficiently demanding.

"I sometimes think," she added, "that being a nun is such a different, independent kind of life that I don't understand as well as I should all this women's liberation business that's going on." I sensed this to be a brand-new thought.

We talked until we ran out of words, yet there were no right ones to connect our planets. Mine had undergone major continental shifts; hers had simply fattened on its axis. Finally, each of us pleaded time.

Walking to the lobby door, we discussed the relative safety of the Hilton's neighborhood.

"I drove through some very depressing sections to get here," she said. "It made me sad to see so many girls standing on street corners."

("Now, girls"—the last footage from the old movie —"there will be no smoking *on* the bus, *off* the bus, or *under* the bus.")

We said good-bye. She waved politely from the steps—a good nun, a strong nun, a conscientious nun, and the Hilton would protect her.

It had been an uneasy reunion, and I felt jumpy from the uncomfortable weather of fondness and frustration that the encounter had created. As I drove away, a stray thought leaped to mind.

I wondered how my perceptions would alter if I were a nun. Would a habit change the world's behavior, making male and female so alike that the streets would seem full of benign influences eager to be of assistance? Would anger lose its edge, innocence gain its footing? Might I not see things quite differently? Or, more to the point, might I not see things as I once had, with the kind of unearned wisdom which precedes temptation?

There must be a reason why Sister Rose had not

changed. Perhaps the culprit was the habit.

"Is this for *The Sound of Music?*" asked the nice Jewish lady at Ronna Costumers.

In a way it was.

My friends were ambivalent. "Suppose you meet a real nun?" asked one of them. "What would you say?"

I searched the corners of my conscience. "If I get run over by a bus," I said, "I'll realize God was against it."

The following morning I rose, put on the rented habit, and backed off from the mirror for self-appraisal. At a distance it washed.

The black floor-length gown was obviously a graduation robe, the belt resembled a drapery cord. But the white cotton helmet covering my hair was authentic enough, the starched bib plausible, and the veil was a separate rectangle of black cloth, the exact weight and weave it should be. Should I pluck my eyebrows? Nuns don't, but I did. Wearing a cross seemed faintly sacrilegious, but I switched my wedding band from left hand to right for an unobtrusive touch of realism. I foresaw that the veil was going to give me trouble.

Altering my day's plan to include hairpins at the drugstore, I peered out the front door, saw that the street was empty, and broke for the car. This is a heavily Catholic neighborhood.

I asked the little Indian girl at the drugstore who occasionally sells me cosmetics where the hairpins were. She indicated the aisle. I picked up a package and brought them to her cash register.

"No tax?" she questioned with a smile. Ah yes—the clergy is exempt. "Uh, I guess." Ringing up the sale, she put the pins in a bag and added, "Everything is so expensive—only rich people can buy." In all my previous dealings with her, she had never been so chatty.

On my way out the door, I stopped to hold it open for an older man who was struggling with an armload of cigar boxes. "Thank you, Sister," he called out with a grin. It was the first time I had been called by my assumed name. It made me feel strong and girlish, as if I had done a wonderful, graceful thing.

One of the fantasies that sometimes kept me company when I was part of a long, dun-colored line of government lunchgoers in a basement cafeteria was to pretend that I was Jacqueline Kennedy. Of course, everyone in the cafeteria was aware of my electric presence, but shyness called for studiously ignoring it.

As Jackie Kennedy, passing a napkin became an extraordinary act of courtesy, waiting patiently at the cash register was a godlike act. Lending the catsup, smiling at the string-bean lady—all those mundane motions of *politesse* underwent a golden transubstantiation. "Isn't she dear?" whispered one elevator operator to another. "You wouldn't think somebody like her would be so nice."

A nun holding open a door is a munificent act of charity.

I got back into the car and attempted to drive a hairpin into the veil.

Obviously this veil was designed for an indoor, wind-free theater. Unless I wanted to maul the material, there was no way to make an easy hole through the veil and cotton helmet beneath and stick them together. Perhaps, I thought, the veil clings very well by itself and, being inexperienced, I didn't know this. I pocketed the pins and drove off. My next stop was a car dealer for repairs.

Whenever I go to the car dealer, the moral dilemma is always the same. Stamp or be stamped on. The mechanics there have a way of breaking the speedometer to fix the transmission, ruining the turn signal while replacing the headlight—the kinds of mistakes you don't discover until you have driven away and they can accuse you of having broken the items yourself.

The chief mechanic was his usual heartless self. As I was waiting my turn behind a man whose problem appeared to be "points," the mechanic was saying churlishly, "Well, it don't make no difference to me—either you get 'em fixed or you drive on out. I don't care." The man shrugged and got back into his car.

"My brother," I said innocently, taking the list of repairs out of my purse, "said to give this to you." The mechanic took the paper, spread it flat on the car hood, and leaned over to read it.

"My brother told me to tell you, sir, that on number five there [the directional light] he believes that it was inadvertently disconnected when you replaced the headlamp several months ago. If you feel this might be true, he wonders whether you might forgo the charge for that particular repair."

I smiled sweetly at the back of his neck, marveled at my sudden lapse into Middle English, and waited. The mechanic mumbled something about "body shop, have to check" and pocketed the list. Nodding demurely, I hoped he understood how greatly I counted upon his honor. The bus stop was a block away.

At 9:30 in the morning, the wind blowing down the avenue was strong and cold, snapping the habit like a flag around my ankles.

Suddenly, what must be every nun's next-to-worst nightmare was realized. The wind jerked the veil away from my head and away it flew down the street. Jesus, Mary, Joseph!

I ran to catch it and saw that it had blown against the legs of two older women walking toward me. Staring at my obscene, ragbound head, they could hardly speak. I was an apparition of Lazarus stumbling from his tomb.

"Oh, Sister," they gasped in concert. One of the ladies took a step forward with the veil. "Oh, my goodness," she exclaimed. "Can I help you?"

I indicated that I needed all the help I could get, but both ladies stood rooted to the pavement, their hands tightly clamped on separate purses. Helping a nun with her habit was much too personal a gesture. Jerking the veil into random position, I said, "Now you've finally seen it—a headless nun." Climbing into the bus, my total effect was dishevelment.

As the bus crawled downtown, there was time to set things straight with discreet little tugs. As if conforming to the routine glances of the other passengers, I was oddly comfortable. Neither then, nor at any time during the day, was I ever mildly overtaken with hysteria. If anything, the habit overtook the impersonator, and quite instinctively I adopted the deportment of every nun I had ever known. For what it's worth psychiatrically, the changeover was frighteningly easy.

A bookstore, an eyeglass repair shop, a cafeteria, a hotel lobby, several museums—I improvised my route as I went along. Because I defined myself as a middle-class nun from a teaching order, I stayed in middle-class surroundings. Then, too, I had no idea what strange thoughts might go through the minds of people on the desperate fringes of the city; I had no desire to be attacked.

I took one cab, two buses, and walked several dozen

blocks all told. Twice I passed by my husband's office, contemplated a surprise visit, but decided against it. Should I ever do anything unprintable in the future, I didn't want any Monday-morning quarterbacking to take place among the staff.

("Well, Mary Frances—don't you remember the day she walked in here as a nun?"

"Come to think of it, Barbara, that was a bit strange, but I never would have thought . . .")

For eight hours I wandered around downtown, a nun on personal business who had no intention other than to complete it and return to the convent by dark. One woman did tell me an abbreviated life story, which I cut short, not wanting to take advantage of her ignorance. Aside from that, there were no desperate souls falling on me with their pain and loneliness. My findings were largely from intercepted vibrations.

When a nun walks by, the faces of older women tend to soften, not unlike the way one greets a pretty child. Their eyes talk about kitchen tables and old friends, the difficulty of being themselves, the disappointments and piecemeal rewards. "I could not do what you do, Sister," the eyes argued, "but we all do the best we can."

"My, you're such a young nun," commented one elderly lady who trudged up from behind. "I'm getting older by the minute"—a flash of inappropriateness too late to retract. "Aren't we all, dear. You teach at Saint Matt's?" "No, I'm a visitor." "Ah well," she said. "I wish you happiness," and, changing her soft old shopping bag from one mittened hand to the other, she walked on.

At noon the streets were busy with young executives in new suits en route to lunch. Their eyes neither approved nor disapproved. Nuns are curious neutrals trailing clean wakes. Every so often, an ex-parochial school boy would cock his head and say, "Good afternoon, Sister," but, for the most part, young men don't give nuns any mental time.

Yet everywhere I went the city was full of father fig-ures—hearty, protective older men with Irish eyes and red noses who naturally and enthusiastically called out, "Hello, Sister," as they eased themselves into bus seats or held open the door. These are the men whose children went to parish schools, who have aunts in the convent, who chafe at guitars during the Offertory, and suspect their daughters but keep their mouths shut. If there was any guilt to feel, it was when one of these bluff, hat-doffing gentlemen made it apparent that he was for me, in principle. As for real twinges of conscience, I was uncomfortable in the extreme only once.

The little Spanish waitresses behind their trays of breaded veal and chicken in the cafeteria smiled shyly, as if remembering something pleasant about themselves of which I had been a part. They whis-pered, "S'ter" and followed me with their eyes as I pushed my tray toward the cash register.

The manager appeared in the kitchen doorway. "Good afternoon, Sister," he said. He motioned to the cashier. "Give the Sister a blank tab."

"Oh no," I protested, "you can't do that."

He snorted with impatience as if I was threatening a long-standing policy.

"Ah, come on, Sister. Say a little prayer for me, will yuh?"

It was either that, or be killed for telling the truth.

As the day progressed, I discovered disadvantages

to being a nun that were unanticipated. My glasses had been turned over to an optician for repair earlier in the day. Without them, I couldn't find the ladies' room in the cavernous lobby of the Mayflower Hotel. Neither could I quite bring myself to ask where it was, knowing that it is popularly believed that nuns don't go to the bathroom. There were several near-sighted minutes and a few false turns into broom closets before I finally discovered one.

My speech underwent a minor sea change as quite instinctively 1 used a breathy, tentative whisper which irritated me. "Excuse me, but . . ." "I wonder if . . ." "Could you please tell me . . ." I approached strangers in the manner of a church usher asking someone to move over in the pew after the service has started.

Yet for all this, it surprised me to realize that for the first time in my adult female life I was looking straight into men's eyes without zigzagging away upon contact. Subway workers, dandies, any man that came into my vision was fair game. Extended curiosity in a nun is permissible. Conversely, men returned the gaze without questioning the motive.

Then, too, the habit offered a dignity which was calming. Walking through the marble halls of an art gallery, I felt straight and graceful, like a second-hand table relieved to be covered with a long cloth. I sat for a minute in one of the interior garden courts and felt the light from the overhead transom warming my chest, ordering my juices, sealing everything tight— paraffin over jelly. By the end of the afternoon, I had perfected a return nod to strangers, a sort of water-pitcher-tipping-from-the-spine action.

The day's experiment came to a close. The cumbersomeness of the long skirt began to outweigh the advantages of gracefulness. Accustomed to striding along in whatever gait matched the music, I was tired of dressage. Then, too, I had been enough places and seen enough people to realize that for all the smiles, and "Sisters," and held-open doors, I had been in the world as a foreigner. I felt wrapped in cellophane, as off limits as somebody else's sandwich on a tray.

While not wishing to change places, people nevertheless overly honored my own. Implied in the tax-free ride was the suggestion that I not stop in transit. Deference altered my ability to solicit information. Kindness was oddly inhospitable at the roots. The world didn't allow a nun to understand; it didn't want sympathy, it wanted a blessing, a snatch of additional Truth. By the end of the day I wanted a convent badly, but it was time to pick up my car.

The bill took the usual overly long time being prepared. Finally, the woman behind the Plexiglas shield (bulletproof, if they're smart) called out, "Sister, it's ready."

I ran my eyes down the right-hand column ($201.55! I'll kill them!). Yet my habit precluded me from giving scandal, and, nodding tersely, I wrote out the check. Naturally they had charged me for their last mistake, which at least proves that the dealer is morally consistent—he'll rip off a nun as quickly as anybody else.

At the intersection closest to home, I tore off my headdress and nosed the car across the rush-hour traffic. A suburban lady from the neck up, it occurred to me too late that I should have negotiated the traffic first. A nun could get away with my kind of driving. As it was, the Irish-looking, older man whose car I blocked getting past was not amused and did something not very nice on his side of the window to let me know.

"I'll tell you something," said the nice Jewish lady at Ronna Costumers as she rehung the habit. "Whenever I meet a nun, I go out of my way to treat her as a human being."

2.

The Bully

In my childhood I was aware of two sorts of mothers: the good ones and the bad. The good ones stayed home, ran the "Funny Hat" parties for the Blue Birds, and prayed for fulfillment, if not in this world, then in the next. The bad ones shopped downtown all day, drank too much, and said to hell with it, but knew in their hearts that they were rotten. The lines were pretty clear. Now, of course, they aren't.

Nowadays no two women draw the line in the same place, and whereas it used to be that distinctions between child-rearing and personal fulfillment were dealt with in the privacy of one's own home, home is no longer an acceptable cover, just as having children is no longer an acceptable *raison d'être*.

Uptown urges and downtown desires—someday they will be straightened out so that the Man-Woman, His Job-Her Job conflicts are resolved. In the meantime God forbid that children should be the first thing people notice about you. There's no quicker route to poor opinion than to be at a dinner party and say brightly at table, "Guess what our Jeremy said today?" Children are taboo at dinner parties, and I can't ever remember hearing a woman say in the presence of other adults, "I am uncommonly blessed to have children." It is more usual to allude indirectly to the fact that we are uncommonly wonderful to have them—given our other aspirations.

This is not to say that I have much tolerance for mothers who perpetually transmit an air of having just blown in from the dime store with a sack full of underpants and can't wait to talk about it. Equally unsettling are those women who study up on kids and are constantly saying unreal things to real children like "Well, it seems to me that you have two choices here, Ronnie," or "It disturbs me to see marmalade on the air-conditioner, Ruth Anne." But judge not lest you yourself be judged—hell, we're all grabbing at straws —and I find it consoling to know that while women are dealing with an overabundance of inspiration, children are present, like so many metronomes, to remind us that a runaway heart makes bad music. On the other hand, who ever consistently loved a metronome?

A recently conducted poll revealed that of the marriages surveyed, the happiest unions were childless. No children added up to no pressure; or, to quote Marlo Thomas's wildly popular (among mothers) record, the childless couple is "Free To Be You And Me." They did not, however, interview me.

If I ever take up with bad companions, stick my head in an oven, or start shooting at cars from a Los Angeles cloverleaf, it will not be traceable to the pressure of children. It is precisely that pressure which has kept rashness at bay. Children do not understand why their mother might want to be an anchorite or a towel girl at Esalen, to go out of her mind or—for that matter—go out to lunch. And it is their very inability to understand which pressures me to shelve these fantasies, or at least rework them on the premises, until I've got my logic right.

It is relatively easy to talk smart and pay out small wisdoms across a downtown lunch table with mere adults. We have been well-trained to accept open-ended theories and tailless abstractions. But children demand much purer explanations of things. In their egocentricity they still consider pain an outrage and parents the exorcists. And as they slowly and instinctually disengage themselves from what is imaginary, who do they look to for confirmation of what's real? Their old fact-weary parents who, unbeknownst to them, are just about to step into the nursery with a few imaginary friends of their own. I call this a blessing, although the giving and receiving is hard work at both ends.

We are sitting together on his bed. The dinosaur book is shut. There are no stories tonight. Tonight my six-year-old son is stringing together the sum and substance of his life, that life which I, being large and efficient and anxious that he leave on time and return on the dot, am unaware of in the main. But the waist-high world of a smallish, shy six-year-old is not an easy place, and tonight I am told of The Bully.

The Bully is someone who notices that you've brought new crayons to school, and he tells you to take them home until you've used up your old ones, and you do it. Quietly, fearfully, and without notice, because "when Ernie says he's going to fight you up, Mom, he means it, and I will always be the loser."

The Bully is someone who makes you give him your bike and the quarter in your pocket, and then makes you follow him on foot to the candy store while he spends your quarter.

That's what The Bully is and there isn't any way around him because he's bigger, has his birthday sooner, and you have the last birthday in the class. These are the facts.

I search through my great books and large themes for some counterfacts, but my insights are obscured by the memory of another Bully—a little girl with finger curls and a smirk who brought crustless sandwiches in her lunch box and whose comic books were in chronological order. I tell my son rather lamely that everyone experiences at least one Bully while growing up. But the look on his face tells me that's not much of an answer.

I tell him other children get their feelings hurt, too, but this is too abstract. A six-year-old's heart is barely large enough to encompass his own misery. I tell myself that I've shot my wad on that subject and had better move on to a new one.

His bike. Maybe we should think about getting a new one now that spring is here and his old bike is about to disintegrate. But he won't let me off so easily.

"I don't like Monica anymore."

"Why?"

"Because when she is playing near me on the blacktop and sees Ernie beating me up, she just stands there."

"Maybe she doesn't understand what is happening. Maybe she thinks you are only playing." He is silent, affixing a value to this latest suggestion.

"I have the last birthday in the class," he murmurs

stubbornly. "And next to Rachel, I am the smallest one in the room."

Smallness. How do I deal with that one? All of a sudden, a neighborhood has been reclassified as a combat zone. Oak trees are thick at the base and conceal bigger boys who leap out and set your heart beating wildly under your T-shirt. The blacktop is an arena and the referee is the teacher—another large person—who is geared to react to outrageous infractions but who wants to drink her coffee or catch a little sun against the wall. Her eyes flick slowly across the bobbing heads like a radar scan on automatic, and she doesn't see that little boy out there rubbing his Keds against the curb—the one who is thinking and thinking but can't think what to do.

It's not all woe. We talk long enough to find a few pockets of hope. Every once in a while, he informs me, he actually finishes up his "hard papers" (all papers are called "hard") before the bell rings and—he looks at me with guarded pride—"I don't know what to do. Should I ask Miss Frazier for more work or what?" He grins and is pleased with himself about this.

Snatching the high note, I pat the lumps out of the blanket, fish the dinosaur book from the sheets, and reach for the light.

"Mom, there's just one more thing."

My fingers rest on the switch. "What?"

"I can't go to sleep because of something else on my mind."

"What's that?"

"It's about that little boy on TV this morning."

It was too much. We had just spent twenty exhausting minutes on truly mountainous problems like bullies, smallness, and being afraid, and now he wanted to know about a little boy on the other side of town, whose parents had cried on Channel 7 and said that he weighed forty-five pounds and was wearing a blue shirt and sneakers when he left home. It crossed my mind, as I searched for a response, that I was being manipulated.

"There are some things"—cornered, trapped, killer of dreams—"there are some things that you can't do anything about. The police are all out looking for him." It was pitch-dark as I lit this bogus candle for his sake.

"But I could go out and look for him," he hurled back. "I know I could find him. I have sharp eyes." The sharp eyes filled up with tears.

We sat together silently, on a darkling plain somewhere between my facts and his fantasy. Finally, I kissed him and turned out the light. He called out to me as I walked toward the door.

"You don't have to be a policeman to look for somebody."

"I know," I said. "I know." But I didn't know much of anything. A ferocious wind of affection was tearing my ribs. Maternalism had overtaken every other instinct. I would camp by his door forever, a large, witless guardian with a spear. Nothing else was as important, and I knew for certain that I would never go downtown again. Well, almost never. Vows, like blessings, need to be reexamined every now and again.

3.

My Father, the Prince

Fathers. They say that a woman seeks—in love, marriage, or any male-female relationship of real heft —to approximate the father she had, the father she didn't have but wanted, or the father minus the attributes that caused her mother to leave him for good and sufficient reason. In the winnowing-out process that precedes deep commitment to a new man, the daughter subconsciously throws up the wheat of her father's virtues along with the chaff of his faults, and her decision to commit is strongly influenced by that first experience of male companionship.

I think they're right.

We all know that men consider their mothers when they choose a woman for themselves, but fathers have traditionally been considered mere linkage in the rosary of wombs that produce progeny from one decade to the next. Accessories to the fact, off-campus providers, fathers are six o'clock visitors to the nursery tended by all-powerful mothers.

One can scarcely overestimate the influence that mothers have upon their sons. But fathers have yet to be properly weighed in as determinative factors in the lives of their daughters. To my way of thinking, this is a terrible oversight.

In a grayer, more small-minded period of my life, I used to inwardly gripe at the inaccuracy of the Cinderella story. Cinderella does not go from ashes to amethysts. In real life the brooms and the dustpans materialize after the wedding, whereupon she spends forever after staring out the window wondering where her father—the real prince in her life—has gone.

Of course, women are now rewriting that old script, and this is an age in which we are forming piano-moving companies, hiking up telephone poles, and swimming along with Jacques Cousteau. But I live with a little woman, aged seven, who recently gave me to understand that liberation is an acquired taste and no substitute for gut feeling.

"What's this?" I asked as she handed me a crayon drawing of a little girl next to what looked like a giant lollipop.

"Me," she answered. (There was a crown drawn on the little girl's head.)

"And what are you doing?" I pursued, searching the drawing for some evidence of a plot line.

"Nothing," she said matter-of-factly. "Just standing by the bus stop waiting for the prince."

I put the drawing aside, looked at my matter-of-fact daughter, and thought with chagrin, "Aren't we all!" Spoiled or despoiled by the first prince in our life, we understand, either way, what it means to be born to the purple. No, Cinderella did not accidentally fall for royalty. Her dear departed father had given her an early taste for it. My father did the same.

He was a tall, crooked-toothed, curly-haired man, who smelled of Lucky Strikes and St. Johns Bay Rum shaving lotion. He was the only father who wore penny loafers on business trips, a Mouseketeer hat to pick up my brother on his first movie date, and had the delicious gall to invite the richest girl in my class (she had her own pool but an exclusive number of invitations) to come on over to the house ("When you're free, of course") and watch our lawn sprinklers.

"Sometimes we get them going in opposite directions to each other," he said dryly, "and it's terribly amusing."

The richest girl in the class laughed nervously, I choked back my borrowed triumph, and savored the fact that once again my father had effectively punched out the opposition on my behalf. He had a gift for it.

Yet, unlike other men blessed with a quick wit and a rare natural electricity of being, my father was oddly incapable of parlaying his gifts to his own long-range advantage.

As I grew older and more able to observe him objectively in group situations, I noticed that in a room full of peers he would usually back up against the mantel and go into a sort of social receivership that did not jibe with my understanding of him. It made me impatient. He was far and away the largest talent in the room, and it seemed a terrible waste to give over the floor to anyone else. Yet he consistently passed up opportunities to reveal himself in public, and it was many years before I realized that my wonderful father was *shy*.

I was thunderstruck. Is Douglas Fairbanks, Jr., shy? Does Cary Grant falter? Should my father have anything in the world to hesitate over?

It was one thing to be a pudgy, preadolescent girl trying to make it in a class full of gazelles, but quite another thing to be that little girl's handsome father, who at various crucial junctures had told her that all she had to do in order to succeed was to take this step, or that action, and—for heaven's sake—was the world such a difficult nut to crack after all? Of course not!

If there was any one thing that my father did for me when I was growing up it was to give me the promise that ahead of me was dry land—a bright, marshless territory, without chuckholes or traps, where one day I would walk easily and as befitting my talents. The fact that I didn't know what my talents were did not put my father off in the slightest. He knew potential when he saw it.

Thus it was, when he came upon me one afternoon sobbing out my unsuccesses into a wet pillow, that he sat down on the bed and, like a strong, omniscient archangel, assured me that my grief was only a temporary setback.

Oh, very temporary! Why he couldn't think of any other little girl who was so talented, so predestined to succeed in every department as I was. "And don't forget," he added with a smile, "that we can trace our ancestry right back to Pepin the Stupid!"

That last piece of news turned out to be true, but whether he believed the rest of his words or not I don't know. He was, after all, gazing down upon a disheveled ten-year-old who was too embarrassed to shift her gum from one cheek to the other.

But I listened to him carefully, and by the time he had finished talking I really did understand that someday I would live among rational beings, and walk with kind, unvindictive people who, by virtue of their maturity and mine, would take no pleasure in cruelty and would welcome my presence among them as an asset. It was only a question of time before I came ripping out of my cocoon, a free-flying butterfly that would skim triumphantly over the meadow of my choice. I cannot say that my father was completely wrong.

Time has passed. Choices have been made. I am no longer a preteen in a net formal who secretly hoped that all the other girls at the Father-Daughter Dance were eating their hearts out. My father's crooked front tooth was replaced several years ago by a nice, straight, shiny one. He has passed through the hospital several times. There are grandchildren. I sometimes think that it is not the same between us, or perhaps it never was what I thought.

One's memory is selective, and I admit that it's to my advantage to recall only those moments when my father rose to the occasion and parted another Red Sea of Impossibility and elbowed me across. Yet these moments really did happen and I am not the same because of them.

There are some people, my father is one of them, who carry the flint that lights other people's torches. They get them all excited about the possibilities of an idea, the "can-do" potential of one's own being.

That was my father's gift to me, and whatever psychic wounds remain to be thrashed out between us are still lying on the floor of my unconscious, waiting for deep therapy to uncover. The fact is that I am closer to my mother. But they say that a daughter carries around the infection of her father for life.

They are right.

4.

In Defense of Children

Several months ago I started a diary, thus quietly joining a long line of men and women who seek to find wisdom, perspective, and insight by jotting down the thrust of their daily lives. It was not my first attempt.

When I was twelve years old, a crashingly dull period of my life, I purchased a bright red leather diary at the dime store and hoped that, by possessing a place to write things down, things might actually happen to me. It was a classic case of putting the cart before the horse.

The pages quickly filled up with lackluster entries such as "Today I cleaned out the parakeet cage," "Sammie Sanford's hamster bit me at her slumber party," and "No school today—heh, heh, heh!" The record of my life was such an embarrassment to me that I saw no need to commit its contents to paper for even one more boring day.

Life obviously lay around the corner, although in those passive, peaceful times, young women had a conveyor-belt sense of destiny, and while the belt moved them closer to the corner, they had the luxury of simultaneously waiting for what lay around it and knowing with some assurance what they were going to find: marriage and children.

I was no exception, but as I leaf through the pages of this second diary, it is clear that the girl who featured herself costarring in a Fred MacMurray movie, rolling toward the beach in an old station wagon, has had to confront certain realities that were only obliquely alluded to in the well-thumbed Baltimore Catechism that instructed me and countless others like me in parochial schools across the land. Yet the fault lay less in my preparation for marriage and children than in my preparation for life; somehow I thought they were one and the same.

The National Organization for Non-Parents (also headquartered in Baltimore) is very clear-headed about "the way life is" today. They take the position that in this day and age the couple who opts for a "child-free life-style" should be given the same sort of hearty applause formerly reserved for the parents of thirteen who used to appeal for baby food on *Strike It Rich*. N.O.N. hastens to say that it is not against children. God forbid! But if you are a "pronatalist" (someone who supports policies that encourage reproduction for all and "exalts the status of parenthood"), you can forfeit your N.O.N. membership, and they are sorry for you.

N.O.N.'s literature is full of surveys, statistics, and grateful letters from couples who were almost pushed over the edge—into parenthood. The famous Ann Landers column, in which 70 percent of her readers came out against having children if they had to do it all over again, is mentioned repeatedly. The literature also refers to a University of Kansas study reporting that the intentionally childless couple, while being no less altruistic or materialistic than other couples, was more likely to show "less interest in interaction with people," have more prestigious jobs, and express "a higher appreciation for personal freedom."

There is nothing like having children to enhance the concept of personal freedom, and N.O.N. has a point, albeit not mine.

There will always be couples who, for good and sufficient reason, choose not to have children. I have no quarrel with them. There will always be couples who wind up having more than they can handle. It is too late to quarrel with them, although they are a good source of babysitters. But where I smell a rat with the child-free life-style people is in their thesis that children make their parents unhappy, that they are to blame (if not personally, at least by virtue of existing) for the divorce rate.

To my way of thinking, this is a little like denouncing vegetables because they won't grow properly in poor soil.

I don't know what to make of N.O.N.'s ultimate position on children. Perhaps I am emotionally blinkered by having them and there is an IUD in my head that simply aborts the issue before it takes hold. It could be that these non-parents feel about children the same way I feel about harpsichords. They are exquisite, but I know I'm not capable of maintaining one in my own home. The humidity isn't right. Or, as one eighteen-year-old girl commented in a piece of N.O.N literature, "Children are fun as long as they're not mine. I've had some very beautiful experiences with children."

So have I. I have also had some experiences that shocked, overwhelmed, and frightened me, such as the afternoon my five-year-old burst through the front door shouting, "Emergency! Emergency!" Rounding the corner, he thrust a drooping daffodil into my hand and screamed, "Quick, get some water. It's *wilting!*"

Yet if someone were to ask me whether I would have children all over again, I wouldn't hesitate to say yes. This is not because I have an excessively romantic view of them, am immune to the call of a career, or live with a man who can't think of anything more fun to do than build rabbit hutches over the weekend. I would choose to do it over again because children stand like immoveable Sequoias in the middle of one's life, daily upgrading the quality of one's thinking, the extent of one's selfishness, and the depth of one's love.

It would be a large untruth to say that children are small sanctifiers whose purpose is to improve adults. Nor are they cheerleaders, urging marriage toward success. Nobody I know feels like that. Children are often the glue that keeps a couple together during sticky periods, but if a marriage is going to be ruined, they will quite possibly speed it along. This is because when two adults are groping for maturity with each other, it's more difficult to achieve this around children, who are even more immature than we are. On the other hand, there are times when one's own lack of maturity is forced to give way simply because, with children, there is only one way to be—mature.

As I read them, however, the N.O.N. people are more mature than anybody. They encourage a new sort of patriotism, in which couples are urged to sacrifice the experience of children so that future generations can procreate with some assurance of being able to pull it off. When society gets its ecological act together, when men's liberation flowers, when the world has revised its day-care tax laws—then we can dare to be great with children again. But selfishly speaking, when I imagine the unlimited free time I would have if children were not present, time in which I could develop my ideas, values, and understanding of life, I seriously question what sorts of conclusions would be forthcoming. So much rich, spontaneous material would be unavailable to me.

Not long ago I was tucking my daughter into bed, and after gazing intensely at me from her pillow, she said solemnly, "You know what, Mommy, I would risk my life for you."

I gave her a big hug, and while we were embracing I answered, "And you know what, Eliza, I would risk my life for you, too."

There was a moment of silence while we digested each other's pledges and then, from the plane of my shoulder, she said, "Mommy, I just have one question."

"Yes?" I encouraged.

"What does 'risk' mean?"

5.

Unsubsidized Women

Once upon a time, little girls were influenced by
books: good books, by good writers, about very good
little girls, or at least very winning ones. If every once
in a while a Jo March or a Caddie Woodlawn (bad
girls redeemed by good hearts) made it into print,
their naughtiness was nevertheless well to the right
of the Natural Law, and sin was almost out of the
question.

I frankly preferred the sinless types, the sweetly
noble heroines who cut through adversity with the hot
knives of their virtue and wound up, like Shirley Tem-
ple, cuddling in Lincoln's presidential lap.

There was always an Abe Lincoln archetype lingering on the periphery of these prefeminist stories,
waiting to catch or confirm these girls. The mixed
message was that yes, virtue should be its own reward, and no, one shouldn't expect the world to lay
five dollars on top of that, but *mirabile dictu*, the
world always did—in fiction.

For some years now I have been pushing my absolutely favorite book, *The Little Princess* by Frances Hodgson Burnett, upon all the little girls in my neighborhood. But there are no takers. Little girls must think differently these days. Yet the heroine of that lovely, undidactic book, Sara Crewe, was the quintessence of what I wanted to become.

Generous when rich, philosophical when poor, neither proud nor toadyish, and always ready to break apart her last hot cross bun and share it with anyone, Sara was a sort of classy Little Match Girl who was curiously above trying to further her own interests. But that was all right. In the last chapter when it seemed as if she must surely die under a thin coverlet, she was rescued from her garret by Ram Dass, a kindly Indian next door, who used to watch her feed sparrows and remarked to his heart that this was a kid who needed some attention. Which she got, I might add, in spades. Or, rather, diamonds.

In all the pre-experiential primers that readied me for life, there was always a Ram Dass who stood ready to bail out the heroine if necessary. Even Nancy Drew, ostensibly a free agent, fell into this category. She drove the roadster but, face it, Carson Drew kept up the insurance premiums.

As for the Dana Girls, they had their adventures, but didn't they always drag themselves back to a girls' boarding school? Now there's a nice, laundry-tagged cosmic certainty, and never mind who paid their tuition. That wasn't important to the plot.

No, my heroines were hardy but not boys, and while my own girlhood was depressingly free of haunted houses, desert islands, and water-filling caves, I did find myself without any money at the ice rink once. But while hungrily eyeing the doughnut display, I

looked up into the kind eyes of a man who gratui-
tously forked over fifteen cents—and I didn't even *ask*
for it.

Not asking was key to my conception of how life
was supposed to operate. I was, after all, a girl. Girls
don't have to ask, because men, after all, are supposed to be on the lookout for that sort of needful situation.

Men were many wonderful things, but I had it very
clearly in my head that they were, first and foremost,
Subsidizers. Provided, of course, that one was a good
little girl.

Well, there must be a lot of bad little girls in this
world today, because communities are filling up with
women who are not being subsidized by anyone. Almost invariably as a result of divorce, they are suddenly without credit or cards, an extra paycheck,
social standing, or marketable skills. And after years of
not having to ask for things, they suddenly find themselves in a no-man's-land where, having extricated
themselves from one kind of bankruptcy (emotional),
they find themselves faced with another kind (financial)—you know, the *real* kind.

These women are the new "Madonnas of the Trail,"
living in a world that doesn't know whether to judge
them as pioneers or malcontents. Nor is there much
literature to support them. But you see them hustling
to the vegetable co-op pickup point before work, walking their children back from day-care centers in the
evening, cursing over cracked car radiators, and puz-
zling over Form 1040's at the kitchen table. Nobody's
"My Little Margie," they are suddenly forced to exercise muscles they are not even sure they possess.
Well, they *asked* for it!

I haven't checked with Gloria Steinem on this one,

but my guess is that there will be a large office party at the headquarters of *Ms.* magazine when it puts out its last issue. They will all celebrate the fact that at last their message, garbled and ungraceful as it sometimes was, finally got across—to men. For one of the reasons that women are getting divorced is traceable to the women's movement, which has suggested that it might not be inappropriate for women to ask men to love them. Not just with their paychecks (although who would turn one down?), but with their hearts.

I am not a fan of unisex fashion trends in which men and women walk about like "Trekkies" in interchangeable clothing. Nor do I have much to say to those thinkers who discount the difference between sexes and would have me romp androgynously along, never noticing that the hand I held was interchangeable with my own.

But there has been one unnatural separation of the sexes that can't go on indefinitely, the old head-heart division of labor, where man is expected to provide all the external support in exchange for women providing all the internal reassurance. It's not fair to either side, and the equation is rapidly being invalidated as more and more women discover that they have heads as well as hearts.

What women are asking men for is a little rearrangement of the commodities, a unisex emotional life where there is a mutual "cash flow" of support between one another. That request is not unconnected with women's newly discovered ability to earn "cash money."

There is something a bit gross about factoring in this last thought that now women think they, too, have earned the right to be psychically supported by a man. But it can't be discounted.

Traditionally men have been entitled to this *droit du roi,* which isn't the same thing as actually receiving it, but I knew what to do when my father came home from work. I waited until he fell asleep on the sofa, slipped his glasses off his nose, took the newspaper from his lap, and uncrossed his legs. And I loved doing it. I still would, as a matter of fact—up to a point.

That point was reached some time ago by many women, and while it would be easy to make martyrs of such women and impale the men no longer in their lives upon that point, it would be dishonest.

The streets are not full of Heathcliffs who got their comeuppance. They are full of men who were educated to believe that men and women, after the rice is emptied from the suitcases, need each other for different things.

In many of the sorrowful, ugly scenes that take place when divorce is imminent, the withdrawing of the credit card signifies that there has been a tremendous misunderstanding. Credit cards are replaceable. The chance to undo the damage is not. And while one could conclude that the woman suddenly on her own is a knee-jerk feminist determined to make up the difference between a full and empty heart by herself, I conclude differently.

Men and women will never stop needing each other, or only at their own peril. But with a little luck some of the reasons will change. It should not devolve upon his cash or her cachet, for, in most instances, it was not the woman's wallet that lacked subsidization, but her spirit.

6.

My Blue Suede Bishop

Many people have found it necessary to say something profound about the death of Elvis Presley. I am just as anxious to say something profound as the next person, but a frantic search has turned up nothing, which would not be the case with Katie O'Reilly wherever she is today.

Katie O'Reilly knew, understood, and interpreted Elvis in the recesses of many a dark living room with a string of boys who wanted to learn what Katie knew. But the fact is that when Elvis was in flower, I was not.

This is not important in itself, except that there may be others out there who, for want of a spokesman, have been too embarrassed to admit the same thing. Actually, there may be quite a lot of us who bluffed our way through the "Fabulous Fifties," and have been suffering through these days since his demise hoping that nobody will ask what Elvis's death meant to us.

To say "not much" is tantamount to admitting that you've never shared a milkshake, held hands, or gone to a movie with a member of the opposite sex. In fact, all three of these things had happened to me by the time I was ready for college. But I must further admit that Elvis had nothing to do with it. He was frankly too Neanderthal for my tastes, and given a choice between Elvis Presley and Dean Stockwell, I would have chosen poorly, precisely because I would have been far too timid to step that far over the line. Elvis was for "them."

This is not to imply a cultural split, but a temperamental one. There were girls, nice girls, in my school who knew how to wangle letter sweaters, ski dates, and class rings from boys as easily as I knew how to play "Oklahoma" on the piano. I admired them in the nonenvious way that one admires Olga Korbut on the balance beam. But it never occurred to me that one could simply decide to switch horses and be the other kind of person. Nor, as I recall, was I ever urged to do so.

My father once cocked his head to one side and asked, "How are you ever going to find a man on the volleyball court?" But he was always kidding around like that, and I didn't take it seriously.

We dance from the soul or dance badly, and Elvis's soul did not match my own. Of course, there is no waste in the universe, and later on he reappeared to dance a veritable tattoo upon my unguarded heart. But that is another story. During the 50's Elvis was simply not present to me, and, while I regret his death and don't think we'll ever see the likes of him again, I would have had a lot more to say had Archbishop Fulton J. Sheen passed away at that time.

Fulton Sheen was a far more influential person in my life. Once a week he swept across the television screen, pounced upon the chalk, dashed a consecrating "J.M.J." across the top of the blackboard, and whirled around to face the camera—cape unfurling, eyes twinkling, and smiling that wonderful smile.

What would the Archbishop be telling us tonight? Would it be a clarifying story about the Trinity, a joke-strewn meditation on the Holy Family, or perhaps a passionate statement about Mary and her place in the world today? One never knew, but it didn't matter. The fact that anyone could make God dance was reason enough to tune back in every week. We wanted to see if he could do it again.

Bishop Sheen shared the same airwaves that Elvis Presley used, although they were as diametrically opposed as the good and bad angels in my mind. "Uncle Fultie" he called himself at the height of his popularity, and there was an endearing "Berle-esque" quality to him. But he was a saint, we all knew that. He prayed steadily for the intentions of great and small alike, and I used to imagine him pacing up and down behind the curtain before airtime, great dark eyes and beaked nose pointing toward the floor as he ticked off his rosary beads and made the world a little safer for Eisenhower, who wasn't even Catholic.

There was nothing small about Bishop Sheen, and it was a fact that television sets were switched on in bars, cocktail lounges and other secular establishments across the country when "Life Is Worth Living" was on. And when he sang out his concluding statement for the evening, in that clear Irish pitch that could knock Gabriel off a cloud, he never forgot to doff his skullcap, bow to the waist, and, in that merry way all holy men have, rise, fling out his arms, and breathe exultantly, "God love you!"

This sounds like a parody. It is not intended to be

one, although I am aware that to admit having been turned on by the swirl of a cape when the rest of my peers were elsewhere in their minds amuses me now. I am simply describing what I saw from a slightly more adult perspective, and given the choice between reviewing the famous *Ed Sullivan Show* where Elvis "did it" for his fans or a rerun of any of Bishop Sheen's shows, I would be very much of two minds. On the one hand, I would be sorely tempted to see what it was that I had missed. On the other hand, I wouldn't want to miss a review of what was once a very real part of my life.

It is easy to forget that during the same period when Elvis was singing "Blue Suede Shoes" and giving Katie O'Reilly the inspiration she needed to work through her adolescence, there were other influences abroad in the land.

Bishop Fulton J. Sheen was one of them, but he appealed to a quieter crowd. His audience was not inclined to form fan clubs, wear identifying T-shirts, or style their hair differently than before. But he had a tremendous impact, although his death did not, in my estimation, get the sort of posthumous play that squared with his contribution. But that's the way it is with the world. Bishop Sheen knew that, and while he had the chance and the sponsorship, he did his level best to explain it to us.

7.

Neighborhood Creeps

Certain books are so wonderful that I can't bring myself to finish them. They "stimulate me"—as James Thurber once commented about a brilliant friend—"to a point beyond which I think I cannot go."

One book that affected me this way was Annie Dillard's *Pilgrim at Tinker Creek*. Now there's brilliance for you! Who would have thought there was a book, let alone a best seller, in exalting the lowlife of a stream?

Her insights were extraordinary and I could only manage a couple of chapters before leaving the book behind in a friend's kitchen. Yet I mentally refer to those few chapters, those few insights, all the time. I think about Annie Dillard approximately 100 percent more than she thinks about me, and just the other day, while wandering up to the corner market for a quart of milk, I realized I was Annie Dillard. The only difference is that she hung around a creek while I hang around a neighborhood. It just never occurred to me that there was a book in it.

What does, or doesn't, occur to somebody explains why some people dine at the Georges V and other people are lucky to have jobs stuffing napkins into cafeteria dispensers. Or, as Annie Dillard commented in an article for *Harper's* several years ago: "I believe that wherever people seek power that the race is to the swift, that everybody is in the race, with varying and merited degrees of success or failure, and that reward is its own virtue."

Around here on the grassy fringe of the city, the "swift" and the "powerful" are already well in place downtown by nine o'clock in the morning. The Social Darwinists would find that those of us left behind— shaking out mops, tweaking off dead geranium leaves, and idly waiting to see what the day will bring forth—underscore their favorite thesis.

We are the lowlife: women, children, old men, delivery boys, retired alcoholics, an occasional creep. All of us, either by choice or circumstances, are out of the race. Or *beneath* it.

A neighborhood relates to downtown the way silt relates to a creek. Life tends to rush overhead, en route to someplace else. Yet power is not measured by the speed of forward propulsion alone, and having been part of this neighborhood's "silt" for a number of years now, I've come to appreciate a different kind of power. But I didn't see it for what it was until I'd hung around long enough.

"Tolerance" comes closest to describing it, "the capacity to endure or accept." Yet that's not quite it. There is an arched-eyebrow quality to that word which smacks of a Christian effort not to pass judgment for the sake of one's lily-white soul.

Truth to tell, people around here pass judgments upon each other all the time. Why, just the other day our dog nearly chewed up the local Brownie leader's rabbit and the air was *full* of judgments. Correct ones, I might add. But by and large we are gentle with each other, and while "little bunnies" routinely get chewed up by "big dogs" downtown, there is a different ethic at work in this cul-de-sac, and I say more power to it!

Living among us are three or four individuals who are here because they literally can't think of where else they could be. Human beings of the lowest cash value in any society, they are the tragically flawed who through no fault of their own were born without everything they needed, specifically, complete brains.

I think first of Harold, a nineteen-year-old boy who only gets off his bicycle to get on it again. Harold thinks he is a fire engine, and you can always hear him coming because he does an excellent siren sound as he whizzes down the street en route to another imaginary conflagration. As far as I can tell, Harold is perfectly content to be a fire engine for the rest of his life.

Every once in a while, he smacks into one of my children with his bike by accident, but I've never heard them complain about it. "It was Harold," they say with resignation, and they don't take the matter any further.

Robert is somewhat less fortunate than Harold because Robert is smarter. It is his particular cross to know, without being able to put his finger on why, that he is not like everybody else, and it troubles him. But Robert is a born helper, and he thinks he is a member of the local rescue squad—a fiction that the rescue squad has not thought fit to disabuse him of.

At every traffic accident, house fire, or downed wire, Robert is there directing cars, warning children away, and being efficient, which makes him feel a part of things.

One time, however, Robert felt a bit more a part of things than usual and he squared up to a pretty teenager down the block and asked her to a rescue squad dance. She could not, in conscience, say yes, and her no confirmed everything that secretly troubled Robert about himself. For several weeks he didn't show up at any fires or accidents, and then he somehow resolved it all and was on the scene once more.

But the most frightening and least absorbent member of the neighborhood is John. It took my children a long time to get used to him, with his unfixed stare, lolling tongue, and trousers that may or may not be fastened on any given day.

We had to have several conversations about the difference between "mental" (which is what the children call each other when annoyed) and "mentally retarded," but even so they tend to cross the street when they see him coming.

John has no errands to perform, no fantasies he can communicate to others, and, for the past five years, no father to take care of him. Every morning he wakes up to the fresh discovery that his daddy has died, and for the rest of the day he grieves over it.

Sometimes he grieves at the playground, other times he drags along the sidewalk, and on the morning I went up the street to buy a quart of milk, he was just sorrowing into the corner market.

Curly Edwards, the market manager, is a tall, strapping black man with an ivory-colored mustache and a head that must be bald because he always wears a hat. There have been times, while waiting my turn at the checkout counter, that I have amused myself by squinting him into an African bishop, a jazz musician, a high-rolling confidence man, a stockbroker. Curly is a man of many parts and possibilities who loves women with a salaciousness too all-encompassing to be anything but chaste.

When John shuffled into the store, Curly was packing groceries at the cash register.

"Hey there, John," he said softly.

John let out a low moan, looked down at his sneakers, and tried to say something. Curly nodded, continued packing the groceries, and answered, "I know John, I know. But you just can't keep thinking about it."

But it is not possible for John to think about anything else. He shook his head slowly from side to side and began again. Maybe Curly didn't understand what had happened. Half sobbing, he tried again, but it was hard work. His tongue wouldn't do the right things. Finally, Curly withdrew his hand from the grocery sack, clamped it firmly on John's shoulder, and interrupted.

"I know what you're saying, John. I know what you're saying. And it's hard to live with. But there ain't nobody who's going to get out of it. Not you. Not me. Not anybody. We're all born to die, John. We're all born to die. Y'understand?"

John was silent. His head hung down over his chest. Then he nodded sadly, turned toward the door, and started to leave.

"We'll see you, John," said Curly. "Just don't think about it." And with one last pastoral pat, Curly took his hand from John's shoulder and plunged it back into the sack to straighten out the groceries. Then John was gone.

This little neighborhood is not particularly noted

for its advanced state of holiness. We rarely wake up with sainthood on our minds. But it is a small enough place that pain and compassion have frequent opportunities to meet each other, and when that happens we are less a neighborhood than a diocese.

There is an insight to be gleaned from all of this, but my mind resists doing the necessary work to capture it. It is enough for me to witness these encounters when they take place, to understand that there is a certain power in them that sideswipes the Darwinists, while not necessarily invalidating them. Dogs do lie down with bunny rabbits sometimes. But you have to hang around long enough to see it. Annie Dillard taught me that.

8.

Integrating Southampton

There was a time when I knew what I knew with great clarity. Then there was another time when what I didn't know poked its foot from behind the curtain and demanded to be integrated—all at once. I was on a train.

Behind was a lawn-cool campus, filled with girls like me—enthusiastic innocents who meant well but weren't quite ready to do anything about it. Ahead was a young stockbroker, my first rendezvous with New York, and a letter home that I was chafing to write as soon as I had something to say. But in the middle lies the story. As the train bore down upon Grand Central, it swept past a broad swath of Spanish Harlem and I was given my first involuntary look at the flip side of the mattress I had always bounced on with such certitude.

Bucket-jammed fire escapes hung off sweat-stained rooms. Angry women in curlers smoked inside. Children ran wildly through alleys spray-painted with obscenities. I saw nothing but junk, poverty, and unsanctified pain. Worse, I had no idea how to fix it, and while I had often asked myself why I should be the one to suffer the indignity of second-hand clothes from rich cousins, suddenly that question reversed itself. Staring at the obscene filmstrip flying by the window, I wondered what I had done to merit a date at the Plaza Hotel. I was forced to utter "nothing." My hands began to perspire.

The first time one slips on a cosmic banana peel is very painful, primarily because it is so unexpected. But as I rubbed my hands up and down the sides of my coat, frantically sorting through index cards in my mind for an answer, the card that kept appearing on the top of the pile bore the face of my uncle Ned.

Uncle Ned was a cool, seersuckered gentleman with quiet eyes, a slow smile, and an existence free of the usual slubs that mar the fabric of other people's lives. His toast came upright on a silver tray, his *Wall Street Journal* was always folded in the requisite four sections for the commute downtown, and, when asked, he had opinions about things—thoughtful, well-researched opinions that always hung together.

I was desperate for a thoughtful opinion before my head blew off, and while I couldn't quite imagine the two making contact, I wondered what Uncle Ned would say if his eyes strayed from the *Journal* to confront the untidy sorrow of Spanish Harlem.

The train arrived at Grand Central before I could get the uncle Ned in my mind to deliver up the integrating solution I needed, and Spanish Harlem lodged itself in my consciousness as a symbol for everything I didn't understand, people I hadn't met, and ideas I was fearful of pursuing. An hour later I was sucking on a swizzle stick, outwardly unchanged. But the fact was that I had almost choked on my first thin slice of life. I was nineteen and a pretty wobbly pilgrim, but the pilgrimage had begun.

I am double that age today, and while I have yet to solve "the Spanish Harlem question," I don't think my uncle Ned is any nearer to solving it than I am. In fact, some years back I realized that he wasn't even trying to solve it, whereas I have taken enough trains and bumped into enough different people that I no longer view Spanish Harlem as a threat at all. This thought has been part of my luggage for some time now and it travels well. It certainly makes train rides more fun, turning the diverse into something to celebrate, and here we all are, catching the curves together.

But the other afternoon, in a noncelebratory frame of mind, I took the train from New York to Southampton and quite unexpectedly stepped upon another cosmic banana peel, although this one didn't materialize until after I had descended from the train.

Southampton is the end of the line in more ways than one, and to be truthful I was looking forward to a little chilled consommé on a private beach. But I was also expecting to laugh at it a little, make my secret jokes about the "Uncle Neds" in their floppy expensive shirts sitting next to women who wore bathing suits that I didn't think they made anymore. Predictably, all the material I needed was there—up to and including a gentleman who did nothing but "hold."

"What do you mean, 'hold'?" I asked the woman next to me.

"I mean," she said with a laugh, "that he has holdings, and he holds onto them for a living."

It was all good fun until suddenly it wasn't. I felt

sad. Looking at the towheaded children, their pretty mothers, the lantern-jawed dowagers, the white-haired men staring out to sea was like looking through an old pre-Spanish Harlem scrapbook, where everything was perfectly clear—like chilled consommé.

At the end of the afternoon, we would take our beach umbrellas away, sit on a white porch, have supper, and read our Ellery Queens until we were too tired to turn another page. It would be so calming and quiet, like the noise that stocks make when they are appreciating in a vault. And, of course, that is exactly what one's stocks must continue to do if one wants to partake of the privileged simplicity of Southampton. It was that illusion of simplicity that bowled me over, made me homesick, made me sad.

The nostalgia did not devolve upon anyone's net worth, but upon everyone's acceptance that there was one way of being, of doing, of looking, of speaking. And while I knew this was not true, I wished that it were.

Of course, I argued, Southampton isn't real life, but then again these people on the beach are real footprint-leaving people, aren't they? In other words, there's something to Southampton, just like there's something to Spanish Harlem. What was exhausting was trying to integrate one with the other.

Lying on the white sand under a beach umbrella, I decided that nobody was asking me to do that, and as I tried to determine how many days it would take before I got bored, I was in no hurry to leave. For the time being, I was content to "hold"—and that, I suppose, is the difference between nineteen and thirty-eight.

9.

Some Easter

Not long ago, I decided to form a group called "Parents Without Promise." Actually, I wasn't sure whether the group would ever materialize, but when I tested out the idea among various friends there was instant acceptance. It turned out that I was not alone in feeling inadequate for my children. There were others who, behind brave fronts and closed doors, sat bolt upright in dark living rooms after everyone was asleep, taking notes on their weaknesses, reviewing dialogues that had gone the wrong way, and contemplating their children (sleeping without the pajamas they refused to wear) who would wake up all too soon, to do battle with and under parents who had made promises (to themselves) they could not seem to keep.

The group has never really gotten off the ground, not for lack of desire but commitments at home which keep us apart. But once every other Wednesday night, two of us regularly meet, my friend, Molly, who has nine children and needs to get out of the house, and me, who has three and cannot leave. We meet at my house.

The other evening the subject turned to "being perfect." I confessed that I approached each day having already lost my own moral justification by 9 A.M.

"What do you mean?" asked Molly.

"I mean," I explained, "that I'm not capable of leading the life I want to lead. In my perfect day I would have risen at six, meditated for a half hour, gone jogging for a mile, made blueberry muffins for breakfast, and been ready when the children came downstairs. And that is only the beginning of the perfect day. I find it difficult to expect my children to take me seriously when I don't have it in me to order my own life well."

"Do you think," asked Molly incredulously, "that anyone leads that kind of a life? Do you also think that in order to be a good parent, one has to?"

"I don't know what I think," I answered. "I just know how I feel."

The rest of the evening was devoted to raising that donkey out of the ditch. But it was a very heavy animal, and we only managed to lift his head and forelegs onto the highway. I am still, given my natural inclination to thrash myself in lieu of changing, stuck in the mud, staring at my aspirations, which laugh in my face from the road.

Take, for instance, Easter. We are a family of baptized Christians, although the bulk of my fervor for carrying out the weekly traditions of church-going expired at the font, and I have never managed to make up for it, even on Easter, a sin of omission that my children, who like Easter baskets as well as the next family, point out to me every year.

This Easter was no different. There were no eggs, no jelly beans, no new dresses and suits, almost no church. One son, the one with the newspaper route, slept through the first move to church, and when the other two children and I returned, the eldest came downstairs to go to a later service. But not before all three of them had served up their discontent.

"I don't like to hurt your feelings, Mom," said my daughter, "but you never celebrate Easter."

"Never?" I said.

"Not for at least three years," she confirmed.

The two boys nodded Their faces looked very sad and—sitting at the kitchen table, reviewing my record —I knew they were right. Nor could I explain this record. Starting with Hallowe'en, moving through Thanksgiving, and culminating with Christmas, I had pulled the family through. But Easter was too much for me. A stubborn, donkeyish selfishness took over. I liked Easter the best of all celebrations, but I never thought that jelly beans had much to do with the feast. But what kind of a parent would cavil over dyeing a few eggs? My eldest son left for church with his little brother, who decided to tag along for the amusement. The house was quiet. I sat at my desk, feeling full of broken promises. Reproach filled the air.

An hour later the front door opened. Immersed in a book, I did not look up until I heard a swish of paper and the two boys crept with odd looks on their faces into the room.

"We got you something," said my eldest son, whose

largest failing seems to revolve around being consistently on the take.

"Me?" I said. "What do you mean?"

He whipped out a bunch of flowers, wrapped in white paper—six carnations, dyed bright pink, blue, and yellow.

My youngest son came up from behind. "We didn't know what you wanted," he said, in an almost reverential tone.

I took the flowers and buried my nose in them. The words of thanks bypassed my throat and became tears in my eyes.

The two boys arranged themselves on the sofa, their eyes wide open with a kind of delight and astonishment that their idea had worked out so well.

"We didn't know what you wanted . . ." they both kept repeating, for want of anything else to say.

And for several minutes, the three of us sat together talking about carnations. But an absolution had taken place and my children, who could not have known this, had put the donkey back on the road.

10.

Philosophical Dirt

My mother was not a good housekeeper, but fortunately she came to marriage with a dowry of inherited antiques that either hid the dirt or fooled you into thinking that a Huguenot had put it there. When she thought about housekeeping at all, she operated on the theory that what is good is clean enough, or could be gotten back into shape if she ever had to sell it; and more than once she has dug up a petunia patch with a rattail serving spoon and not thought a thing about it. This philosophy infected me early on.

My predilections for housekeeping run along the lines of "what you don't see won't embarrass me," and although a clean house is a joyful thing, the manpower to get it that way is still, in this semi-evolved world, woman.

Go ahead. Slam down your fist on the table and cry, "What about him?" But does your fist come back to you covered with honey butter? Housework is a sticky, genderless reality that does not wait while one is at the negotiating table, and at various times during my career as an unpaid domestic, I have experimented with different attitudes of mind, all the better to get the job done and still have a little time for a magazine on the chaise longue.

It should be mentioned that I rarely put first things first. The good book tends to come before sluicing the carrot peelings down the sink, my feeling being that one needs to be "up" for the carrot peelings; and a brief peek into the *Letters of Abélard and Héloïse* gives me momentum, something to think about other than the gnashing action of the garbage disposal. As for housework itself, I find that I must revert to philosophizing or self-delusion, which some people think are one and the same thing.

One ruse is to pretend to be a trembling new maid reporting for her first day's work at Jackie Onassis's New York town house. It puts me into an entirely different place, and suddenly I am wandering around the house trying to determine how clean is clean, if one could afford to make up the difference.

"Mrs. Onassis likes the grout between the bathroom tiles cleaned with a Q-tip dipped in Pine-Sol," instructs my phantom superior. "And don't forget to scour that garbage pail with baking soda before inserting a fresh liner."

In this particular fantasy, fear is the driving force. As I nervously stitch back loose alligators on John-John's shirts, I am thinking that, with luck, I may be able to fly in the rest of my Irish cousins from potato land—if only I can prove myself. But unless I really throw myself into this act, I find I am fighting off another fantasy which tells me that I am Jackie Onassis, and right about now I should be sitting in the living room reading Truman Capote, or better yet, talking to him.

On several occasions I have attempted a fantasy blend and donned stockings, pearls, and my only leather skirt, as if to impress upon the dirt that it should be an honor to be scooped up by someone so refined. However, the only profiteers from this trick are the dry cleaners, and upon thinking about how most people approach dirt, it seems that they have a philosophy that either facilitates or obstructs.

The Romanticist thinks she is misplaced. This floor, that pile of laundry, those unmade beds can't possibly be the stuff of Real Work. We should all sleep, Heidi-style, on a tick in a hayloft. Real Work would be hard but photogenic (shearing sheep, sowing seeds, plucking grapes), tasks performed away from offensive appliances and miracle fibers that commercialize or seal up the good earth. In other words, because Armstrong, not God, made linoleum, she eschews it. It shouldn't even exist. In the Romanticist's house, linoleum lies under a cloud of unknowing dirt.

The Mystic takes an altogether different view. She drops to the linoleum like a nun taking vows. It is the road to salvation, her particular rugged cross, and she clings to the hope that on the Final Day, God will call her blessed, even though her husband never got around to it in this life. I think this particular mindset is quietly going out of business. One still finds sweet prayers on wall plaques, but "Madonna of the Kitchen" statues have not been selling well outside the Boston area.

The third sort of housekeeper is, for want of a better word, a Bureaucrat. Her head is a compendium of useful information pertaining to stain eradication, laundry shortcuts, wood preservation, and fluffiness agents. Her puppy is either trained in a week or drowned, and where she has the jump on the rest of us is in her ability to understand where dirt can hide: over door jambs, underneath high-chair seats, behind the dryer—places the rest of us didn't even know existed. Nonbureaucratic women are very threatened by this kind of housekeeper, and it certainly doesn't help to find out that she has just finished *War and Peace*.

Perhaps these types are caricatures (I've tried them all and none of them fit forever), but no less so than my favorite housekeeper—a poetess who lived and created in perfect harmony with her political-philosopher husband. Her verses on the joys of a swept hearth and a polished heart are widely quoted. Yet a gentle delving into the realities of her life revealed that she was served, from sunup to sundown, by an old-maid sister.

It was the old-maid sister who saw to it that the laundry moved and the cookies were in the jar, and that her versifying sister was served breakfast in bed. When the old-maid sister died, the poetess followed her in jig time, proving the theory that a good domestic is hard to find and some women would rather die than be without one. Yet this is somewhat dancing above the painful point.

Nobody who has spent any extended time shuttling back and forth from one corner of the house to the other can deny that unabated housework is a brutalizing experience. But to pluck a strand from each of the philosophies above, perhaps a rope to swing on can be braided.

One doesn't have to love linoleum but simply view it as legitimate turf. One doesn't have to be a religious nut in order to understand the symbolism of being cleansed through humble tasks. Neither should meticulousness be shunned, since order depends upon some vision of perfection, even if it's only Jackie Onassis. Finally, one doesn't have to be totally absorbed by housework to understand that creative work is done best in an ordered setting—a fancy way of saying that it's hard to sew a ballgown if you've mislaid your pins in the breadbox.

But when all is said and done, I am of the opinion that one either grasps the trick of good housekeeping or one doesn't, and there is a Plexiglas shield that divides the two kinds of people forever. We can stare at each other, but that's about it. The ultimate trick is to be happy about whichever type you are, to understand that God made a lot of different kinds of apples, and it is entirely possible to have a full wastebasket and a full heart simultaneously.

We all need each other, if only to criticize.

II.

Secondhand Living

When I was new I wanted new things, although "wanted" does not convey the passion with which I ripped the cellophane off sock packages with my teeth, buried my nose in the soft flannel folds of my first Lanz dress, rubbed satin hair ribbons across my upper lip, and tossed discontentedly on unironed sheets, dreaming of the canopy bed that my parents did not think was crucial to my spiritual development.

My parents thought a lot of things weren't crucial to my spiritual development, although they did not withhold store-bought items out of a warped desire to keep me simple in a complex world. But my mother could never wear a new dress without saying, "Oh, do you like it? Thirty-nine ninety-five at Livingston's," which somehow took the sting out of the purchase, and my father (in between Chris-Crafts) liked to hang around the U & I Trading Post, a junk shop that specialized in gravy-stained neckties and cracked Caruso records, on the odd chance that *The Letters of Olive Schreiner to Havelock Ellis* might turn up in a bin.

My parents had a disrespectful attitude toward new things, which cut across the angora sweater-charm bracelet ethic that prevailed in the rest of the neighborhood. I would sit all day envying Diane Sach's latest translucent retainer, which she clicked in and out of her mouth with casual satisfaction, and try to make my own retainer with paraffin and rubber bands.

But at night I came home to a house full of slipcovers that never hung right because the slipcover lady couldn't work without being plastered on cream sherry, and would feed the zippers through the machine at a drunken angle yelling, "This is idiot's work!" at the top of her voice.

With such a background you either develop a lifelong commitment to glass dining room tables and the integrity of B. Altman & Company, or you decorate your walls with birds' nests in crates, prop your feet on the coffee table that used to be a carpenter's box, and hope that you don't become a caricature of yourself any sooner than the next person.

It is my belief that people who don't like used, secondhand, or even trash-picked things are not going to be convinced to change their minds by someone who gets hot flashes in Sloane's. In fact, it would be too bad if they were dissuaded. Do we want a world in which everyone is in love with birds' nests, or can't look at a tree stump without thinking "chair"?

No, we don't, although having made a pitch for different tastes, I confess to being uncomfortable in houses that are store bought, modern, and coordinated. It affects my thought processes. I feel compelled to think in abstract, nondenominational terms, to sweep the decks of my mind to prepare for Buckminster Fuller and a string of modern ideas that my secondhand, second-thought mind cannot handle in such an angular light-struck environment.

In fact, I cannot handle Buckminster Fuller in my own living room, which is full of odd tennis shoes which comfort me with the realization that there is less to life than the geodesic dome. But a thoroughly modern house irritates me, as if I were in the middle of a planned community that had sprung up overnight without tradition, trees, or old people sitting around on busted chairs to remind you that life is too short to be spent carefully aligning this month's magazines on the table.

Having dispatched the opposition, I should hasten to add that a house that relies on chewing gum to keep the candles straight in their holders is not my idea of heaven either. But whoever avoids used, abused, or overlooked items when furnishing an environment is missing out on the chance to bring character, eccentricity, and the spirit of other people now passed on into his or her life.

When I open bureau drawers and inhale old sachet, I am consoled by the fact that I did not get there first. The bureau comes with ancestors who used Friendship Garden talcum powder. They aren't my ancestors, but this is the nuclear age. One can't be choosy.

The best junk shop in my city is a rank, lime-colored warehouse called "Value Village." Half the clientele jives around the aisles with transistor radios to their ears, and the management doesn't take checks, which says something about who goes there, I suppose. But the Ritz-Carlton doesn't take checks either, and the glory of Value Village is that you can find some Ritz-Carlton buys that satisfy one's desire to steal without risking the police blotter.

My last purchase was a hooked rug for $29.50, which I brought home, rolled out on the front-hall floor and waltzed around, in love with its colors, dignity, and price tag. I cannot imagine a more perfect rug, and its value is enhanced because it has been somewhere else before. I am not responsible for imbuing my rug with all memories and associations. It is fully developed, like the pair of golf cleats I almost bought for $2.50, which I imagined to have been ripped off a heart-attack victim on the ninth hole while his feet were still warm. I lingered over those golf shoes, but couldn't think what to do with them. They were too specific to put on a coffee table, and I wasn't quite brave enough to mount them on a wall. I regret my lack of bravery. They were gone the next time I was there. But I picked up a 1937 chrome-perfect Remington typewriter, which now sits on the dry sink below a pair of prints that my mother gave to me the last time she tried to simplify her life.

My house looks a lot like my mother's house, which is a comfort since I am my own mother so much of the time. Everything is used, faded, full, and familiar. Every once in a while I pour beeswax over everything to enhance the flaws, which don't shine as well without polish. I am at home with flaws. They remind me of me.

12.

Dreams

My mother is not an ambitious person. She never gave a fig whether any of us came home with A's or married rich, which as things turned out was fortunate. Nor is she unduly concerned over life's little downhill runs, those situations (like the time my second cousin eloped with a walnut picker) where most people would draw back and be justifiably purse-lipped. Mother is sane, but not to a fault, and while she is perfectly aware of those areas in our lives that she hopes we will someday clean up, greatness in her view has its own gestation period and could theoretically descend in the last ten minutes of life—which is one of the beauties of her outlook.

Thus it was that we regularly trooped home with rotten report cards, disappointing friends, and muffed chances, knowing that Mother wouldn't hold these things irrevocably against us. "Defeat," she used to say, "is nothing more than a learning experience," and while there were those outside the family who secretly thought that life required our family to learn from setbacks more regularly than most people, I don't agree. Looking back, we were simply more verbal about them, and in times of adversity Mother would gently urge us to reconsider the acorn. She was a great one for acorns and mustard seeds, where all is dark until one day the light reveals what has been going on all the time.

Yet it would do Mother an injustice to portray her as a dippy metaphysician, even though just the other day an old envelope full of seeds she once mailed me fell from a book. She had forgotten to tell me in the accompanying letter what the seeds were, and when I checked back she said they were giant Sequoias. Sometimes Mother is off base. But although she is an eternal optimist, I would give equal weight to both of those words in order to avoid classifying her as an ersatz Peter Pan who has never bumped into a sorrow worth mentioning. She has had plenty, but that is not the point. How she has dealt with sorrow when it arrived is. And it seems to me that it has everything to do with her receptivity to sorrow's reverse, joy.

Joy is not a word that we flip out across the lunch table very often. It is a private sort of word, encountered even less often than spoken of. But once experienced, we are changed. That is, I think, because joy is the unforgettable by-product of having one's deepest intuitions confirmed, one's most secret hopes validated, that part which fantasizes itself most valuable suddenly set free. Ordinarily it takes us by surprise, like a trumpet voluntary in an empty church that we had originally entered for the dreary purpose of trying to get it all together again.

Getting it all together is what joy needs in order to

operate. For whatever the cause, joy is preceded by that swift organization of the parts into a whole, where suddenly what we thought was just a dream translates itself into a reality, and then we are left with the dilemma of how to keep it together. For once that kind of integrity is experienced, it is very difficult to settle for anything less. Unless . . .

Anyone who has pushed off from an insight and tried to turn it into a reality knows it is a costly trip, and the streets are full of people who have decided that the trip isn't worth it. After all, where will it end? And will anybody be there when we arrive? These are not small considerations. And if one chooses to re-trace one's steps, there is at least some consolation in knowing that you've avoided suffering the conse-quences endured by the other people who have chosen to make the trip. Dreams cost.

It has been said, however, that what we first dream of becoming, minus some of the outlandish trappings with which children cloak their intuitions, is the first clear indication we receive of who we are. The heroic mood, explored within the safety of an oak's elbow, the dancer's heart, molded in the updraft of a swing —these early spin-offs mean something.

But there is something very deep within most of us that checks our earlier impulses to trust life. Upon being told, for instance, that I was pregnant, I could not shake the conviction that I would probably give birth to an acorn squash, and it was only when a per-fectly beautiful child was held before my eyes that I had faith in what had gone before, which is no faith at all.

Yet how a dream turns out depends very much upon ourselves and our faith. We can choose or not choose to follow it, and while this implies a certain something out there that we must capture or perish, in the long run we are really deciding whether we want to be ourselves—the authentic, handmade original that exists behind the compromises made to fit into the world without getting in anybody's way. That kind of a choice is not a one-shot deal, but a consistent series of choices, and who among us has the energy, let alone the courage, to do that?

Courage is one of those commodities we think we have until we need it, can't find any, and lapse into despair. But courage is, according to psychologist Rollo May, "the capacity to move ahead in spite of despair." As if that weren't sufficiently paradoxical, Dr. May adds that the highest types of courage involve being "fully committed, but we must also be aware at the same time that we might possibly be wrong."

My mother claims that she made plenty of wrong choices in raising us, citing as her chief error the fact that she tried to protect us when she should have been much more tough-minded, which was tough to do. But in one way she has been very tough-minded all along. While always managing to convey that there was something very valid and original in each one of us, she always stopped short of telling us exactly what it was. For one thing, she did not exactly know. For another, who we were was our business. She was simply optimistic enough to believe that one day we would know, and if choosing to honor it entailed more than a little sorrow along the way, well, that was the sharp edge of any dream.

13.

The Call of the Soil

When I was small, I dreamed of large things: magic carpets, personal press conferences, an invitation to have my feet immortalized in the cement outside Grauman's Chinese Theater. These things did not materialize. When I grew up, I continued to dream of large things: a change of circumstances, absolution for sin, the chance to be in a room full of people where everybody understood exactly what everybody else was saying. These things, for the most part, did not materialize either.

This is not to say that I proceeded to fall in love with unfulfillment. But after the stars had outwitted my butterfly net for a sufficiently instructive period of time, I lowered my eyes to the earth and listened to Emerson. "There is a time in every man's education," he wrote, "when he arrives at the conviction ... that though the wide universe is full of good, no kernel of nourishing corn can come to him but through his toil bestowed on that plot of ground which is given to him to till." I became a gardener.

It should be said that this was not my first choice of things to become. Of course, any man or woman who gardens and hears another person say that gardening is not one's first choice will feel, at the very least, compassion. But chances are he will keep his compassion to himself. The call to the soil is a powerfully individual call, pivoting upon a readiness that cannot be given one to another, and while some people may simply pick up a trowel one morning and never put it down again, that certainly was not my case.

I have avoided the trowel since birth, considered the earth something one was morally obligated to try to rise above, and when I suddenly intuited that my salvation might lie directly underfoot, it was an uneasy realization. I didn't know anything about the soil, and if that was where salvation lay, it looked as grim and unpromising as the semifrozen, untilled plot of ground which spread itself beneath my inexperienced feet last April when the call to gardening came. Fortunately, I was not standing alone.

Mr. Olson, a tall, tooth-perfect seventy-three-year-old with long, white curly hair that he keeps mashed into place with a baseball cap, was by my side. The self-anointed, unchallenged "president" of the local neighborhood garden cooperative in which I sought entry, he was mildly encouraging as to my chances of getting in.

"We've got eighty plots this year, and more applicants than spaces," he said. "But if Mr. Schummacher drops out, on account of his heart condition, we might be able to squeeze you in. In any event," he continued, "you'd best come to our first meeting this

Friday evening at the Nature Center. It'll show everybody that you've got the proper interest."

That Friday evening some fifty or so people gathered for a slide show in the Nature Center's auditorium. A small, nervous man from the Park Service was on hand, to give the city's imprimatur to the gathering, but he hung in the background with a stack of forms. It was Mr. Olson's show.

"Here is one of the best zucchinis from last year," said Mr. Olson, flipping a picture of an outrageously large zucchini, arranged sideways on an upturned laundry basket, onto the screen. In one appreciative exhale, the audience breathed "aah."

". . . And those of you who were part of the cooperative last spring might remember Mrs. Ridley's red cabbage." Onto the screen came a smiling Mrs. Ridley, kneeling beside a monster of a cabbage, her hands supporting its furled head, the way women do when being photographed with their first babies on a back stoop.

"Of course," added Mr. Olson, his tone turning wistful, "not everybody did right by their gardens." Onto the screen came a scruffy, weed-choked plot, all lamb's-quarters and dandelions, with a few stunted tomato plants trying, against the odds, to grow. Who could have allowed such a thing? To let one's ten- by twenty-foot parcel go so entirely to seed? The audience was silent.

"We're going to monitor the plots very carefully this year," said Mr. Olson (at which point my mouth went dry), "and that means no chemical insecticides that aren't on the approved list."

I understood. Everybody understood. As the slide show continued (Mr. Olson wound up the whole thing with a view of Hong Kong harbor at sunset, which was his way of indicating that God really ran things and we should all feel grateful that anything grows at all), we sat in the dark, planning our seed purchases and hoping that the Japanese beetle, which can turn an entire garden to lace in a single afternoon, would keep on flying.

Of course, at that time I did not know about the Japanese beetle. In fact, I was entirely unsure as to how one even prepared the soil for the eggplant seedlings which, God willing, would not succumb to their jaws. And on the first day the garden opened, I showed up with a hoe, a trowel, and a pair of gloves only to realize that I didn't even know how to rake.

Did one pulverize the soil or merely rearrange the topmost layer? Was there a proper equatorial direction in which to draw the rake? Stones should be tossed out, but what about dirt clods? Mulch? The proportions of mulch? What *was* mulch anyway? I was chastened by my lack of expertise, and for several days I knelt humbly on the earth, picking up information from other gardeners who were digging, hilling, and marking off their prospective rows with the string I had forgotten to buy.

Preparation was everything, but as the hours passed I found I had become totally absorbed in kneading this fragrant, mysterious stuff called earth. We were getting to know each other, crumbling our differences, clod by clod. Time flew.

"Your dirt looks very nice," said Mr. Olson, who came up behind me on the second afternoon of my labors.

"Thanks," I replied. "All my life I've wanted someone to compliment me on my dirt."

Mr. Olson is not a man given to cocktail-lounge witticisms, but together we perched on the fence bordering the garden and talked about how inexplicably unpopular the Jerusalem artichoke is. Then the Park Service representative came striding across the garden, redfaced, agitated, and with something very much on his mind.

"Mr. Olson," he said hoarsely, "I see you have narrowed the paths from five feet to three."

"That's right," said Mr. Olson, looking over the tree line. "We don't need that extra two feet."

"Now see here, Mr. Olson," he said. "I can't have you changing things around like this. I've got records. The plan is on file downtown. We can't act independently, you know."

Mr. Olson continued to squint into the distance, saying nothing.

"You'll have to change them back," said the man from the Park Service, who could not deal with the silence but knew he had the obligation to make himself crystal clear. "Why, if the other garden cooperatives catch wind of this, then it's my neck."

Message delivered, he walked away. When he had reached a fair distance, Mr. Olson slid his eyes sideways, opened his mouth, and said quietly, "You ever hear such nonsense?"

"You should have quoted him that passage from the Bible," I said, "about narrow is the gate to heaven, but wide the path to destruction."

This reply took Mr. Olson, who passes out Gideon Bibles to prisoners in his spare time, slightly aback.

"Do you know where that comes from?" he asked.

"The New Testament," I ventured.

"Matthew Seven, verse thirteen," he replied, after which we chatted about the Gideon Society, and Mr. Olson urged me to look into Fourth Presbyterian, or a particular Baptist charismatic church which he understood from others was doing some very creative things.

That is how it all began. A plot of earth, a packet of seeds, and a nervous stomach. In April, with the first seeds just into the ground, I had nothing to show for myself but good intentions and a somewhat childish desire to be a credit to Mr. Olson. The air was cold, I was just a caretaker for some invisible carrots, and day after day the sun hung behind a cloud.

My intellect told me that what is down must grow up. But my heart only partially confirmed this piece of intelligence. Would the cauliflower ever see sunlight? The snapbeans ever climb the pole? I did not know, but it occurred to me that if I invested too much of myself in this garden, I might stab myself with a trowel if the rabbits ate up my lettuce one night. It might be one of the more original suicide notes: "Found in her hand was a piece of paper on which the deceased had scrawled, 'The bunnies did it.'"

But win, lose, or draw, I was committed. I don't remember when I have ever felt quite so excited. Well, actually, that's not quite true. But in this instance, it was a contained excitement, jacketed like a seed within the soil. And looking at that brown raked square laid out with string, I realized that I was really nothing more than a custodian to a mystery that was beyond my comprehension. I think that's what hooks one on gardening forever. It is the closest one can come to being present at the creation.

14.

Bicycling Toward Wisdom

One of the first life decisions I ever made, at an age where causal connections between life and decisions were pretty foggy in my mind, was to switch my college major from English to philosophy.

"Philosophy!" yelled my father over the telephone. "What kind of a job are you going to be able to get with a philosophy major?"

Job? What job? That was a causal connection I hadn't made yet and my father had a point, even though it seemed awfully soiled and commercial.

"The whole point of philosophy," I countered patiently, "is to learn how to *think*. I'll think about a job later." Of course, all indications were that when it came time to find a job, I would have found a husband first, rendering my father's worry moot, but he didn't know about my fallback plan.

"Why don't you be a dietician?" he continued. "There's good money in that, particularly for women."

87

I laughed, told him to relax, and hung up the phone.

Well, as it developed, neither of us was exactly right. The thought of analyzing the nutritional properties of apricot pudding continues to leave a bad taste in my mouth. But to think that one can analyze all of life's problems out of existence by thinking is a fallacy that has trapped me within the Square of Contradiction (a case of freshman logic I never could get straight at the time) too often for comfort. Fortunately, a dazzling little book entitled *A Guide for the Perplexed* by E. F. Schumacher, has recently helped me out.

Mr. Schumacher divides all the problems that assail humankind into two large categories: convergent and divergent. A convergent problem, such as how to build a bicycle, is solved by designing and assembling all the parts and putting them together in the right way. But a divergent problem, such as how to reconcile justice with mercy, doesn't lend itself to this solution. Justice and mercy will contradict each other forever, and the only way to solve the contradiction is to transcend it altogether and wait for wisdom, which sounds quite restful until you think about it.

Everybody is supposed to be waiting for wisdom one way or the other. But how one waits—patiently, impatiently, or, in my case, by staring catatonically at a wall plug and hoping that something will occur to me—separates one human being from another. Metabolism has something to do with it, but as the twig is bent, so grows thee.

I come from a family that believed in rising early, sniffing the wind, and, after they realized that it was impossible to reconcile train schedules, golf dates, and my aunt's decision to paint all the wicker furniture before dark, usually decided to "wait and see what the day will bring forth." That philosophy dovetailed with what everybody wanted to do anyway, and while we didn't exactly stand frozen before the mantelpiece all day, neither did we map out Easter vacation before Thanksgiving, or have a clear idea over breakfast of what was going to happen after lunch.

After all, anything could happen and anything often did, which made life interesting and inclined me to believe that the best way to deal with life's contradictions was to go into an empty room and sit with them until I was on the brink of a nervous breakdown, at which point the telephone would ring and the person on the other end would clear it up for me. Only recently have I discovered how anti-American a belief that is.

Almost no one goes at problems that way, a realization I have been late coming to because most people are too busy to stop and set you straight. In fact, "being busy" turns out to be the universal antidote to grief, sorrow, ambivalence, and general malaise.

When I think of all those philosophy books where "busyness" wasn't even in the index, it is easy to feel cheated. Perhaps Kierkegaard was driven to write about "leaps of faith" because he was too whiffle-brained to do anything more constructive, like clean out the garage.

After listening to enough people tell me that they solved all their problems by sorting through papers, quiltmaking, even reconciling their bank statements in the midst of heart-cracking sorrow, I began to think I had it all backward. Could the general be solved by focusing upon nothing in particular? It seemed a bit strange to think that one could solve a divergent problem with the tools used to solve convergent problems, but perhaps it was possible. Why not? I, too, would bicycle toward wisdom and give busyness a chance to work its boring magic upon me.

Armed with this new insight, I arose one morning and made a long list of things I would do, purposefully factoring out all light-bulb-staring time in the process. It was a long list filled with such items as "replace windowpane," "call dentist," "deposit check," and "clean out attic." I felt a little like throwing up, but I had no place in my schedule for it, and before 9:30 in the morning I had already cleaned the house, done two loads of wash, called the gas company about an overcharge, watered the flowers, planned dinner, and was moving toward the front door, coat on, ready to attack the town with my simulated needs. Then the phone rang.

Under normal circumstances that would have been a source of joy. Someone at the other end had been moved to solve my life. But these were not normal circumstances. I was impatient to get on with my list, and apprehensive that the crisp, businesslike mantle that I still wore a bit insecurely might slip off my shoulders and leave me staring at the light bulb again. But I answered the phone.

"Are you busy?" asked a good friend, not knowing what she was saying.

"Well, actually, I was just on my way out the front door."

"Okay," she answered, "I'll be over in a few moments," and she hung up.

Obviously she had not heard my crisp rejection of her intrusion. Her ears were pretuned to hear what they would hear, and when it didn't materialize she had gone deaf. It made me laugh. I took off my coat, threw my list on the hall table, and went back into my unnaturally clean kitchen to wait for her arrival.

She came within the half hour, all smiles and good feelings, carrying a basket of flowers. Her eyes were brimming with divergent problems, and within the hour we had laid some of them out on the kitchen table and made headway with a few. It felt right. There was a close, comradely feeling that had I been at the hardware store, measuring glass, I would have missed for all eternity.

At the end of the morning she rose from her chair, smiled warmly, put her arm around my shoulder, and said semi-apologetically, "I hope I haven't kept you too long."

"No," I said. "I'm glad you came. But actually—and I know you won't believe this—I'm supposed to be very busy today."

"What do you mean 'supposed to be'?" she asked.

"Well, I got up this morning and made a list of things I had to do, and when you called I was just on my way out the door to do them."

"Oh, I'm sorry," she murmured. "I didn't know."

"No," I answered. "Don't be sorry. It wasn't meant to be." And after she left, I sat down at the kitchen table again, stared at the light bulb, and tried to remember where I had put my list. I would have to start again tomorrow, but in the meantime there was nothing left to do but wait and see what the day would bring forth.

15.

Fear of Families

My grandmother, who spent the last part of her life upstairs thinking about everything downstairs which she could no longer control, was my first teacher about life. Not life as I knew it, or life as it might be in the future, but life as it used to be when men wore kid gloves and asphalt was just a gleam in God's bad eye.

Thus when my gun ran out of caps, the drugstore hadn't replaced last month's comic books, or my imagination needed a fresh dollop of energy to pole-vault over another flat afternoon, I would knock on Grandmother's door, pull up a footstool, and pressure her for more details about her fabulous past.

That past, which largely revolved around a tea table where she accepted and rejected proposals of marriage, seemed to short-circuit for Grandmother around the age of eighteen. But within that span was everything I needed—love, disaster, fancy balls, and a string of ancestors with whom Grandmother had had countless dialogues, all of which she remembered, up to and including the punctuation. It was soap opera before television, and within the script were characters I could never hope to meet in real life.

Great-uncles who ran railroads, great-aunts who ran great-uncles, various duel-prone cousins who fought each other for the honor of taking Grandmother to tea—I had no idea I was related to such dazzlers—and after an hour of mentally gliding around under a lap robe in a Pierce-Arrow, I would emerge from Grandmother's room feeling quite rich with possibilities. Maybe I was an aristocrat who had been trapped in Sears, Roebuck by mistake.

"Of course, you know," my grandmother once remarked, "that you are a fourth-generation Californian." I nodded, unsure as to how one could convert such knowledge into cash.

"What's a fourth-generation Californian?" I asked my father.

"If you were here before that," he replied, "you would be a Digger Indian."

Well, as life has unfolded, I have come to feel a great deal in common with the Digger Indian, and where once I worried about being able to get out of Sears, Roebuck, I now worry a lot more about being able to get in. As for my family tree, the majestic elm which was supposed to shelter me from catastrophe, I have revised that assumption to fit the facts. It's not exactly every man for himself yet, but it's difficult to think of a branch of the family tree that wouldn't break if I tried to swing on it.

Then, too, while trying hard to make decisions, be

mature, and otherwise create a reputation for being a credit to MasterCard, it does not help to remember that one comes from a family one of whose members used to throw the dishes down the bank on the maid's night out. Where once I laughed, now I do so nervously, recalling one embittered in-law who used to slice the air with one hand above her wrist and whisper hoarsely, "I haven't got one drop of your family's blood in my veins."

As life goes on and independence becomes necessary for survival, pride of family can turn into fear of family, and during this past Christmas and New Year's season, which I celebrated with a number of other people's relatives, it appeared that fear of families is not a unique problem. To sit around a table with all those faces that give back the truth, the whole truth, and quite possibly nothing but the truth about ourselves, can give one a "so help me God" feeling.

Twelve months of apartness culminating in a week of togetherness can turn a family reunion into a family face-off. The odds are that somebody will 'say something," a stiffness will descend over the table, and several people will excuse themselves to make early plane reservations home. At one family dinner it got so hot that I retreated into the kitchen, only to be followed by a couple who squared off before the microwave oven, where he said to her, "You want to know what really tees me off about you ... ?" I went back into the dining room where his mother had just said, "Well, I don't think that Sadat acted like a politician but a statesman!" To which her mother replied archly, "And what's wrong with that?"

There were a lot of small vignettes like these going on all over town during the holidays, and the first con-

clusion to draw is that relatives are better off not relating to each other if blood is going to gush all over
the rug. But I can't help but think that beneath all the
double-edged remarks and devastating toasts was a
lot of anxiety that had no place to go.

If the son is threatened by his mother, so also is
the mother threatened by the son. Her loneliness, his
unwillingness to identify with it, his guilt, her bitter-
ness—this is only one of the combinations that sit
above and below the salt, and I wonder whether family reunions don't turn into disasters so quickly because we're only willing to relate to each other when
it's safe.

To embrace the whole of another person is to take
the risk that their dam will break and overwhelm us
with responsibility and anxiety. To recognize another
person's frailty may somehow sap whatever strength
we've managed to build up for ourselves. The anger
comes from sensing that the support we need is not
so different from the support the other person needs.
But to acknowledge that is so painful that some people would rather drink themselves into the bottom of
a bottle of Old Grand-Dad and count the hours left before everyone will go home.

The strain of not relating is what provokes the
bloodshed, and some people will kill each other for
love, particularly during the holidays when we're supposed to love each other to death. But perhaps the reason it's so hard to relate is because it's so hard to be
disappointed, to know that the schizoids, compulsive
cleaners, alcoholics, and dullards, all the relatives
who come home to roost, are not so different from us.

To embrace them is to embrace these tendencies in
ourselves, which is a difficult task. And so anger de-

flects love, hands are clenched behind backs, and we walk the tightrope of the holidays praying the wrong prayer for the wrong reason instead of saying, "What the hell, we're all in this together . . . and while we're at it, let's throw the dishes down the bank."

16.

Maggie's Wedding

One Saturday the neighborhood went to a wedding. It had been a long time since anybody on the block had gotten married. In fact, over the past several years the block had been hit by a distressingly high number of separations and divorces. These, plus the deaths of Bertha and Bernie Topkiss, the resident "grandparents" on the street, who died within six months of each other, had made holes in the neighborhood, and the Topkisses' middle-aged, unwell daughter, Connie, who lives alone in the house, cries often. She is afraid of being alone.

It has been a hard several years for a lot of people, and poor old Mrs. Galvin, a retired schoolteacher who loves nothing better than to stand outside her house and run good news up and down the sidewalk, had begun to think that all the good news in the neighborhood, which sits on the grassy fringe of the city, was permanently gone—or moved away—like the Murrays.

The Murrays, with their eleven children, had moved to the suburbs, vacating the house that we bought. There hadn't been time to know them well, but I had often wondered how life was treating them, and whether their eleven children were still as uniformly friendly, bright-eyed, and full of parochial-school normalcy as I remembered.

I had asked Anne Murray how she managed such a large brood so efficiently. "Well," she said, "I guess you could say that Joe's the head and I'm the heart." I guess you could say that this remark depressed me, although it didn't depress my regard for the Murrays. They came to the wedding along with the rest of the neighborhood, which had been waiting for the big moment for weeks.

When Maggie Hannapel, the twenty-one-year-old daughter of Ray and Ann Hannapel, sent out invitations to her wedding, Mrs. Galvin finally had something to crow about. Everybody did, although I didn't expect my throat to constrict the instant I saw Maggie at the far end of the cathedral nave, or become a complete waterworks when she stepped, in a satin swish, over the chapel threshold itself. Perhaps it was the trumpets.

I am a sucker for trumpets, with their clear, triumphant notes that leapfrog over all rational arguments, depressing conclusions and secular second thoughts, to announce that there is another dimension to life which the accordion, no matter how well played, cannot convey.

Of course, a trumpet in a backyard is one thing—the notes are splayed out, diluted, picked off by the wind. But a trumpet in a Gothic Episcopal cathedral, where each note is snatched up, separate and angelic, to collect like silver in the rafters, is quite another. A cathedral is designed to receive a trumpet, as it was now receiving Maggie, although given Maggie's everyday, backyard image, which runs to cut-offs and her father's old shirts, I had never thought of her in a cathedral context before.

But that's just what the trumpets were saying. This was not everyday. We were witnessing a culmination of days advancing down the nave, and when Maggie stepped into the chapel, looking pink and near tears and leaning hard on both her mother and father who escorted her toward the altar, the entire neighborhood dove for its handkerchiefs. In part for Maggie, in part for her parents, in part for ourselves.

Lined up in rosewood pews, the neighborhood had the brief luxury of transcending the facts of our separated, divorced, bereaved lives to be part of a joining. Trumpets are appropriate for joinings. Maggie and Paul would need all the trumpets they could get, given what Mrs. Galvin always refers to as "the times."

It was an extraordinary service, mostly because it was not too extraordinary. The vows were exchanged while the couple faced each other, both hands clasped, repeating what they had written themselves. Maggie's capable forearms would know dishes and babies. Paul's forearms would know them, too, if Maggie had anything to say about it. But there were no jarring innovations, the congregation didn't have to do anything outlandish, and the ceremony was both Catholic and Protestant, with a priest for each faith in attendance.

There was a brief moment of quiet, during which one of Paul's fireman buddies got up and said something too moving to remember. Maggie's father spoke, but I only remember the tone of his voice—husky. What went on during the service is not engraved in my mind, except that it wasn't an event as much as a confident stating of convictions, and when the couple turned and walked back down the aisle together, the congregation spontaneously broke into applause. Then came both sets of parents. The audience really clapped for them—loud, hard, and sustained. The emphasis was right.

"They didn't kiss each other," complained my nine-year-old daughter, who had never been to a wedding before and felt she had not quite gotten her money's worth. In fact, I think they did, but it was over with so fast that my daughter, who had instructed me to tell her when to hide her eyes so she wouldn't have to look, had missed it.

But the reception entirely satisfied her preconceptions of what a reception ought to be. There was a rock band, flaming shish kebab, Coca-Cola, dancing, and a giant wedding cake, which all the children circled like wolves for the duration of the party.

Maggie lost her slip in the conga line. Her younger sister, Monica, played Pachelbel on her cello. One usher, an enormous, suspender-strained fireman, rolled around the dance floor to "Rock Around the Clock" like a beach ball of happiness. Maggie's father was moist-eyed throughout. "I feel so full," he said.

Maggie's mother kept eyeing the chef, who was engaging in some creative pyrotechnics over the shish-kebab pan.

"If the flame goes too high," she worried, "the sprinkler system in the hall will go off." The management of the hall had rules about shish kebab, but it was too late to do anything about that now.

I saw Mrs. Galvin talking to Mrs. Murray. "I think this one will last," she said. "Oh yes," said Mrs. Murray, "they're very good kids."

"I don't even remember my own wedding," Mrs. Galvin said. "We didn't have a rabbi—just a justice of the peace."

"Oh," said Mrs. Murray, "our daughter is marrying a Jewish boy from Connecticut this fall. They'll be married by a justice of the priest—I mean *peace*—too."

Both women laughed. The times were changing, weren't they?

"Is this the first marriage not in a Catholic church?" asked Mrs. Galvin.

"No," Mrs. Murray answered with a smile, "not the first." Her face had more lines in it than I remembered. Lines of expansion.

"Well," said Mrs. Galvin, patting her hand, "you never know what's going to happen. Why, we've got two adorable Chinese grandchildren."

I left them topping each other's stories and sat down beside my daughter, who was sitting, solemn as a Charlotte Brontë heroine, in a long dress at a table watching the passing parade with a sharp eye.

Suddenly, from nowhere little B. J. Murray appeared in front of her, thirteen years old, in a sport coat, a tie, and a respectful expression. He actually bowed.

"Would you like to dance?" he asked her.

The nine-year-old stiffened and looked over his shoulder.

"No, thank you," she said very softly.

"Oh, come on," I urged on B.J.'s behalf. "It would be fun."

"I don't know how to dance," she said out of the side of her mouth.

B.J. moved gracefully into the void.

"I don't either," he said with admirable honesty.

But she wouldn't be budged. After B.J. had left, I

said, "Well, even though you said 'no,' isn't it wonderful that the very first boy to ask you to dance in your whole life is so handsome?"

She nodded, too overcome to speak. But several moments later she leaned forward and said, "I'm going to wait for you in the car."

"Why?" I asked. "Are you afraid he might ask you again?"

"Yes," she said, and in a twinkling she was gone.

I repeated this anecdote to Connie several days later when we were comparing notes on the wedding. For the first time since her parents had died, she laughed. It was a real laugh—deep, unencumbered, and delighted. I vowed to find more stories like this last one to pass on.

In all the months I had been dealing with Connie's tears, it had never occurred to me that anyone could make her laugh. That, I suppose, is why I am such a sucker for trumpets. At the sound of the first clear notes, what doesn't usually occur to me suddenly does.

17.

Mother's Day

Years ago, before I became a mother and consequently too busy to be much else, I volunteered briefly at a local old people's home. I mention this activity not to bang my own drum. I am attracted to old people, particularly when they are good and old, which is a dazzling combination. But Mrs. Benson was senile, or on the verge, and the only request that invariably wiped the glaze from her eyes and lit a candle in the middle of her soft, slack face was when somebody asked her to talk about her childhood.

Then her face would spring to alertness, her speech, which was usually wandering, became articulate and fully of whimsy. All one had to do was to prompt, "Tell me about the time you lost the muff your papa gave you on your birthday," and she would be off and running, backward, through a maze of lost meadows, hair ribbons, and china dolls.

I would listen with one part of my mind, which was

103

interested, but wonder with the other part whether one day I might wind up like Mrs. Benson myself. Ideally, I should like to burn my candle straight down to the end of the wick and then snuff out. But at the age of eighty-seven, might I not be tempted to let go of the branch and collapse upon a pile of old snapshots?

Even now the temptation to revert to my childhood is fairly strong, particularly since I have become a mother and am a soft-hay target which exists to absorb the excess passion that my children cannot contain. Childhood is remembered because it is passionate, and when I look at my children, I am reminded all over again of how it felt to feel everything, which is the cross of childhood that later on, if we are clever or dishonest, we turn to gold.

My oldest is almost an adolescent. I send him out the door to school every morning aware that I don't know very much about him at all, which is how he wants it, except at bedtime, when he relaxes into candor, and for a few darkened moments I can reach across the divide and communicate a measure of hope.

Someday, I tell him, his confusion will end and the hormones that send him leaping sideways at the kitchen table will arrange themselves better and he will not be at the mercy of those ferocious moods.

The middle child, a girl, is intensely psychological. She thinks in terms of relationships, popularity, bruised hearts, and telephone calls which patch things up between her friends. She is deeply solicitous of me. Her worry is that when she becomes a teenager, she will be obligated to hate me, like a heroine in a Judy Blume novel.

I tell her that it's not necessary to hate me, but it wouldn't be the end of the world if she did. Her eyes tell me that it would so be the end of the world, and the only time she tried to run away she collapsed in tears by the front door, too frightened to make the dash for freedom, too worried that I might not care if she did.

But the youngest is a born rider of the rails. He thinks up reasons to run away, just for the thrill of it, and every day when I kiss him good-bye on his way to school, I automatically say, "Come right back at three," to forestall any inspirations he might have to check out Pittsburgh on his way home. I look into his face, as if to memorize his features, and know that I am not very good at not knowing where he is every minute of his life.

This is a neurosis I am not proud of, but the left hand, which is trying to disentangle my apron strings from his fingers, doesn't know what the right hand, which is trying to lace those strings through them, is doing. Last Mother's Day, however, he got away from my apron strings altogether.

The night before Mother's Day there were broad hints passed around the table by the two older children that tomorrow morning I would be happily surprised by what they had gotten me as presents. The youngest didn't seem to have an agenda. He was silent at the table. Then they went to bed.

The next morning, around six, my daughter came into my room and said, "Justin's not in his bed." I sprang from my own, assuming he had gone downstairs to watch television. He hadn't. I called out through the house. No answer. Was he hiding? I looked everywhere—under beds, in linen closets, and finally outside.

It was a Sunday. Nobody was awake. The streets were quiet, his bicycle was on the porch, and my thoughts were jumbled. The empty bed, the flung covers, the shoes he did not stop to put on—any other time of day I could find reasons for his being gone. But at 6 A.M. on a Sunday, Mother's Day (how macabre), I could find none, and after arousing the household and sending everyone up and down the streets and alleys for twenty minutes of shouting, I went to the telephone, dialed the police, and lived out my worst fear—I put in a missing child report.

The police were instantly solicitous. "Somebody," an officer said, "will be right over." I put down the telephone and tried to think where else he might have gone, or why. There was, I dimly hoped, one more possibility—my garden, four blocks away, in a neighborhood cooperative. I could think of no reason why he would want to go there. He had never gone by himself. But it was the only place I hadn't tried, and getting in the car I drove slowly toward it.

First block, nothing. Second and third, empty, too. But at the end of the fourth block, walking toward me with his head down, I saw him. He was in his pajama bottoms, with bare feet. I slammed on my brakes, flung open the car door, and felt every valve in my heart open with relief.

"Why?" I asked, as he got into the car. He began to cry. "Where did you go?"

"To your garden," he answered, now breaking into a full weep against the dashboard. I took him into my arms and felt his small-boned, warm completeness against my ribs.

"Why did you go there?" I asked.

"Because," he sobbed, "I woke up and remembered it was Mother's Day and I didn't have a present. And I thought maybe I could find some flowers to pick. But when I got to Oregon Avenue, I remembered I wasn't allowed to cross it by myself."

The thought that he was actually afraid of his mother on Mother's Day appalled me. I tried to tell him—remembering how when he was born I thought he was the most perfect, translucent creature I had ever beheld—that I did not want any flowers.

Holding him tightly, I assured him that nothing in any drugstore or flower garden could ever mean as much to me as he did. And wasn't he smart, I added, to remember about not crossing Oregon Avenue. But we had better go home and tell the policeman that everything was all right.

"The policeman?" he exclaimed, looking up, his eyes wide open.

"Yes," I answered. "When I couldn't find you, I had to call the police."

His face took on an intensely interested expression. The tragedy of Mother's Day had been supplanted by a more interesting plot line which kept him bolt upright on the seat as we drove home.

I am certain that each one of us will have a snapshot to remember of that particular day. But in this instance, despite the fact that I am not a child, mine will be the more passionately colored. I looked over at his face, which was alert with curiosity. I could not see my own. But I knew, from the heat I felt, that a candle lit it up.

18.

Adversity Becomes You

One bright blue day this autumn, on the corner of Forty-sixth and Broadway, the X-rated center of the universe, two street musicians were playing to a large, receptive crowd. One played a zither, the other (when his strings weren't popping loose) played a guitar, and both of them, like most of the audience, could be summed up as being more or less "on the skids."

But if misery loves confirmation, it wasn't showing up in the songs being requested. Over and over again, people were asking for G-rated tunes full of waltztime optimism about couples on two-seater bicycles, wearing tulips, down by the old mill stream.

"Can you play 'Harvest Moon'?" asked a thin, belt-less man who looked like he had never witnessed a decent harvest moon in his whole life. The musicians complied, and the man listened with something like yearning, gratitude, and innocence written unself-consciously all over his face. These emotions, in broad or short strokes, were written plainly over quite a few of the faces in that crowd, confirming a paradox I have seen confirmed before.

People who have been slugged by some kind of humbling adversity tend to be more transparent and humanly responsive than people who, for want of a real problem, tend to retreat behind their good fortune and become opaque, which is a problem in itself.

Does this fly in the face of Gloria Vanderbilt's approach to life, which she recently articulated on a radio show as having no time to squander on people who did not have something positive and life-enhancing to contribute, specifically to her? I don't know. It was a cursory discussion. The interviewer did not exactly plumb the depths of her philosophy, and, as I recall, Miss Vanderbilt gave equal time to deploring the common use of the word "hopefully," which is bad English and I guess not life-enhancing, although hopefully she will never catch me out using that word. But she gave me something to think about, namely the question of what is or is not life-enhancing, and while there are different jokes for different folks, it seems to me that the Russians are right.

Sorrow, Russians traditionally taught their children, should be welcomed as an honored guest. Adversity is a teacher. Pain is for something, namely you. A life free of these things is a life that has not been truly blessed, unless comfort is what we're after, and I question, for myself as much as anybody else, whether comfort isn't the greatest temptation of them all.

What feels good, particularly after feeling bad, is to not feel anything at all, which is one way that comfort could be defined. Soft chairs, colors, skin, and life: if the hammock holds, stay in it. But most of the people I know who have been dumped out of that hammock are far and away the most life-enhancing people I know. Adversity becomes them.

I think first of a woman who, if she wasn't an admitted alcoholic, probably wouldn't be admitting much else in her life either, good or bad. But she has avoided opacity by not being able to avoid the fact that she is, without Alcoholics Anonymous, a drunk. She is very funny about herself, honest about a lot of things.

The other alcoholic I know I probably wouldn't know at all if he hadn't finally admitted that he wasn't capable of touching a drop without falling on his face. It is a very elegant face. I can only take his word for it that at one time he routinely behaved in a very inelegant way. He did not begin to write seriously until he stopped drinking, and that is how we know each other, through books. He extends himself to many people now, which he would not have been inclined to do in former days, to people who drink too much but "hopefully," if he can exert some gentle pressure, will admit to alcoholism as he did, and get on with their lives.

I don't know many people who are trying to get on with their lives by seeking out hard chairs. Certainly I don't. But when was the last time anyone with a real problem rang the doorbell of someone who has never admitted to having one? Who, when feeling miserably imperfect, seeks out a perfect person in order to get through the rest of the day? Misery does, in many ways, love company or confirmation. Two minuses do make a plus. Misery exists. What is most uncomfortable is not to have that reality embraced, for purposes of getting beyond the fear of it or, so it seems to me, whenever I've been tempted to run.

Running reminds me of football and a man I don't know very well at all. This friend was a football player, a very successful one, who in his thirties became a mogul in the sports world, and the last time I saw him he had never fumbled a ball in business, his personal life, or any other way of which I was aware.

I bumped into him in the hallway of a school where I was waiting to pick up a child. He, too, was waiting, although in the past ten years he had thickened slightly all over and looked different enough that I had to squint a little to put the face and the name together. Finally, I recognized who he was at the same time that he recognized me.

He walked over with a smile on his face. In his arms he was holding a little girl. "This is our youngest," he said. "She's our autistic child," he added, giving her a protective squeeze as she continued to weave slowly back and forth in his arms.

His face was not the face I remembered. It seemed clearer, less complicated, more accessible than it had ever been before. I did not know him well enough to ask certain questions about how that child had influenced his life. But it wasn't particularly necessary. I could see quite a lot without asking any questions at all. He held his "adversity" in his arms, willingly, without any complaint, although I imagine that, given his impatient Irish temperament, he has had his moments of wishing things were different, very different.

But as he walked down the hallway holding his daughter, I looked at him from the rear and found myself silently congratulating him on his good fortune.

He had been chosen to become more than what he might have chosen to become on his own. It occurred to me that, in various psychological or emotional ways, he could have refused that burden. But he had embraced it and, like his little girl, the burden had become a part of him—the part I admired most as he walked away.

19.

Just Married

One day this March, when everybody else I knew was sorting through canceled checks and feeling frail about their capacity to follow through on their commitments, my seven-year-old son bounded lightly into the front seat of the car after school and whispered into my ear, "Guess what! I just got married."

"To whom?" I whispered back.

"Kate," he breathed, summing up the rest of his life in one syllable.

Who was Kate? Until this moment, a two-syllable charmer called Courtney had always won the sweepstakes for my son's heart. But hearts change. The streets are full of people cursing the same lilac bush that last year had confirmed their deepest longings. Courtney had been aced out, and I looked beyond the windshield for a tiny "bride" who might be standing coyly by the front bumper holding an invisible bunch of stephanotis in her victorious hands. I saw no one who fit the just-married description.

"Was there a minister?" I asked, wondering, given these noncommittal times, just how orthodox the ceremony had been.

"Yes," he whispered, "Brian."

I didn't know who Brian was either, but apparently the "marriage" had taken place on the tanbark during recess and Brian had officiated.

"Congratulations," I offered, forgetting to add, "I hope you will be very happy." But judging from the expression on his face, which reminded me of a restaurant critic experiencing the combination of cayenne and cinnamon in his mouth for the first time, happiness wasn't quite the point. This is a child who wants to get lost so he can ride home in a police car, who once rigged his own classroom expulsion to the principal's office because, he explained, he "just wanted to see what would happen."

Bouncing around on the front seat of the car, he could not decide at this juncture whether he ought to let the rest of the car pool, now fully assembled behind, in on his escapade. But it wasn't necessary. The word was out.

"Justin kissed Kate," announced his older sister, who isn't necessarily against that sort of thing. She herself is in love with a sixth grader, although being of a more conservative temperament she shares that love with her best friend, and their infatuation is a silent, eyes-lowered affair. Their hearts jump when he smiles at them in the hallway, but they mince right by, clutching their integrity, and do not acknowledge anything at all.

"Ha, ha, ha," jeered Justin's older brother, who would rather kiss a python than admit that girls have any place in his life at all. There is one eleven-year-old, a holdover from summer camp, who telephones him faithfully at least once a week. But he rarely takes the calls, not being ready for a natural blonde who carries a teasong comb in her back pocket, and fortunately she lives two bus transfers away, which has put that romance on hold.

I'm not ready for a blonde with a teasing comb either. We are still struggling over the phonic system and how to look up words in the dictionary. But I had been thinking, with my pediatrician concurring, that we wouldn't have to look up the word "love" for a few more years.

Afternoon gave way to evening. Evening gave way to night. The "marriage" was not mentioned again, and by bedtime I had almost forgotten the whole thing. But I noticed when I bent over to kiss the "groom" good night that his head looked a little off-center on the pillow.

"Is anything the matter?"

There was a short silence as the head on the pillow rocked uneasily back and forth with the question.

"I don't think I want to go to school tomorrow," he said in a small voice.

"Why?" I pursued. "Is the work starting to get hard in class?"

"Yes, that's it," he said. "I just can't concentrate on what's happening. My mind always wants to *drift*."

I hadn't heard him use that verb before, although he seemed to pounce on it like a life raft that would float him past responsibilities he couldn't negotiate. For several moments we talked about how that often happens, how you have to tell your mind to "get back on the horse," etc. But I could tell that his mind was drifting ever farther down the river even as I spoke.

"Wait a second," I said, interrupting myself. "Does your drifting mind have anything to do with your getting married today?"

"I didn't really get married," he replied in a desperate tone of voice. "We just walked around together."

"You mean," I persisted, "that you didn't actually propose to her?"

"No, no," he said, his voice climbing into the falsetto range as the truth came out. "I didn't give her a ring or anything."

"Aha," I said, "but you told everybody that you had gotten married, and now maybe you wish you hadn't."

The dam broke. There were tears and denials and a lot of writhing around under his quilt as he wrestled with the consequences of his own foolhardiness.

"I just know I'm going to be teased, the whole class is going to follow me around tomorrow. I'll be the laughingstock, and so ... I'm not going to school tomorrow, and that's final!" He clutched his quilt around his neck and looked at me with as much finality as he could muster lying down.

There are times when one feels less like a parent than a retired brigadier general trying to offer advice to a buck private who has never been to war. You review old campaigns, try to pluck certain strategies from your files, and then—with as much tact as possible—suggest that Plan A might be more effective than Plan B—under the circumstances. This was not one of those times when such a plan came to mind. I saw no alternative, short of facing the war head on. But I promised, as I left the room, that I would give his dilemma my best thinking overnight.

Promises, promises. The next morning I still had no diversionary tactics in hand. But my son arrived at the breakfast table dressed for school with a look on his face that led me to believe that either he had forgotten about being "the laughingstock," or he had come up with a plan of his own.

I said nothing until he was on his way out the door, and then my curiosity overwhelmed me. I caught him by the sleeve and asked, "What are you going to do about Kate?"

He looked at me with mild irritation, as if he did not find the question very relevant, given the fact that this was a brand-new day with the entire beach still empty of his footprints.

"Oh," he said, pulling his sleeve away, "I'm going to give her to Matthew." And that, I assumed, was that.

But that afternoon I picked up the plot the moment he walked into the house.

"Did you do it?" I asked.

"Do what?" he asked back.

"Give Kate to Matthew." (I was beginning to feel that I was the only one who cared about this whole transaction.)

"No," he said, "I traded her."

"For what?" I asked, wondering how many bales of cotton a day-old bride fetched these days.

"For Courtney," he replied and then, with a sigh of exasperation, he added, "and now I just don't want to talk about it anymore."

I had heard that one before, although not from a seven-year-old.

20.

Cheap Thrills

Not long ago I met a man, an astronomically rich man, who had spun so much straw into gold that he was forced to reverse the process in order to have a good reason to get up in the morning. Having already assembled the wine, women, and air-conditioned houseboat on the Rhine (these were luxuries that had long ago been converted to necessities—appreciated with about the same fervor that other people feel for indoor plumbing), he found himself increasingly compelled to be more original about pleasure, if pleasure itself was not to elude him in the end. His latest venture, the one he regaled me with, was a case in point.

One evening a brand-new idea for fun came to him. Within several days everything was in readiness. Boarding one of his planes, he got it halfway across the globe, landed it in Timbuktu, and for five apparently unforgettable days and nights, rioted in the desert with assorted stewardesses and pilots.

They staged camel races, drank beer, and—this last detail fractured him—hung the empties on a couple of beat-up cactus plants nearby. Nobody bathed, nobody combed, and at night they rolled up in dirty blankets (loaned out by some puzzled Timbuktu natives) and slept it off under the same stars that had wheeled above Antoine de Saint-Exupéry. "I can tell you," he chuckled, "we had ourselves a ball."

We drank to that "ball" with a second cup of Blue Mountain coffee, yet gazing at him over the rim of my cup, I couldn't help wondering, "What does one do after Timbuktu?" It seemed to me that the finger would have to press pretty far into the flesh.

The pursuit of pleasure can be a complicated business, one man's holding company being another man's subsidiary. But there isn't anyone who doesn't have a private list of cheap thrills, those Barcaloungers of the mind that receive us when life won't. That's the utility of a cheap thrill—if life doesn't pan out, at least we have the consolation of knowing we haven't spent our entire time crying over an empty jewel box.

Time was when sitting between two friends at recess could propel me through the rest of the day. Now it is enough to know that I have two friends. The day I learned how to crack gum is a day I remember. Transferring buses, looking blasé—these were some of the brief, biodegradable pleasures that came and went like smooth stretches of sidewalk under my roller skates, and casting back to one of life's early intolerable situations, Shopping With My Mother, I developed a cheap thrill which ultimately allowed me to go downtown by myself.

Stiffening up one leg, I began to limp. Looking down, my mother saw what I was doing, became irritated, and said, "Stop it!" I did not stop. She yanked my hand and pulled me forward. "I said stop it!" she repeated. Several pedestrians shot wrathful looks in my mother's direction. Affecting an "I'm trying as hard as I can, given the fact that I'm a cripple" expression on my face, I pretended to comply by moving my stiff leg a little faster. It was a no-win situation for my mother (the entire street was on my side) and the whole thing delighted me. Sometimes when alone downtown I would stiffen my leg again, just to cash in on a little free sympathy from people who didn't know what a faker they were holding the door open for. There's a rip-off artist in everyone, and just the other evening I caught my ten-year-old son ripping off time itself.

His eight-year-old sister was prattling on to him about some event in her day. I looked over at him and saw that he had hooked one arm over the kitchen chair, pushed himself away from the table with one foot, and was gazing at her with a certain avuncular mixture of amusement and ennui that was perfectly synchronized with the arm, foot, and tilt of his body. He was playing at being a teenager, a cheap thrill if ever there was one. I averted my eyes to preserve his privacy.

At one point, plotting the geographic location of every boy I had ever kissed, and sighing with relief that they would never meet one another, constituted a thrill. Walking down Fifth Avenue and knowing that I would definitely not have a nervous breakdown has shored me up. The little mind games we play while waiting for something significant to happen all constitute cheap thrills, and while my current list wouldn't make a seminarian blush, they take my mind away from what might surely strike me dead tomorrow and serve as small, peeled grapes that nourish me today.

Thus, while worrying about financial insolvency, the mere act of looking at my American Express card cheers me up. Other mornings I wake up and get dressed as if I had a regular job at Time, Inc.

Reading a magazine during plane takeoff is satisfying—the cheap thrill being the knowledge that I have evolved beyond the primal scream. Thinking about the fact that Annie Dillard chain-smokes inexplicably fortifies me, and when I feel entirely nailed down and incapable of moving one foot beyond the precincts of the neighborhood, I have sometimes driven a few blocks away to a corner drugstore fountain, bought a magazine, and a cup of coffee and pretended to be someone from out of town who is marking time between important appointments.

I suppose that some people might think these little pop joys, like buying a new belt for the vacuum cleaner and running it over a week's worth of whatever is on the rug, are rather pathetic. But all things are relative, and if it takes Timbuktu and a case of beer to satisfy my rich acquaintance, he could not have been anymore exhilarated than my daughter when she recently broke her arm.

The break itself was neither cheap nor thrilling. But the next day was a different story. She went to school with a new plaster cast, and while the cast would have been sufficient in itself, clutched in her other hand was a *pièce de résistance*—a fistful of birthday invitations.

For one brief moment, she had it all: pity, admiration, envy, power. That particular cheap thrill bordered on joy, and sometimes they do resemble each other. I suppose that one of the tasks in life is learning to discriminate between them. Otherwise you might wind up in Timbuktu.

21.

The Trouble With Rachel

There are in this world certain children—you are either one of them, or their victim—who crop up in every new generation like dandelions to bedevil the grass. They are not evil, perhaps not even calculatedly malicious, and seen from the heights (which is how most adults view children), they aren't even very exceptional. But what do we know? More to the point, what do we remember? There is at least one baby tyrant in everyone's past—a slab-toothed gloater who ruled the class with the moral authority of a person whose socks never slipped down into his or her shoes. Who knows what miracle glue these children possess?

There is one pale-eyed eight-year-old in our life at the moment whose power is so tremendous that the mere lemon wedge of her smile can set my daughter dancing until bedtime, transparent with joy because "Rachel likes me."

On the days that "Rachel likes me," we are bionically self-confident. There is no box too heavy to lift from the dock. But on the days that "Rachel hates me" or "Rachel can't decide," life is not worth living, all confidence evaporates, and this means that you fall down twice, get an eyelash in your eye, ask for tuna fish and get ham in your lunch, and no one wants to be your partner at recess.

Recess, as anyone with half a memory remembers, is that barbaric interlude when the Rachels of the school choose their courtiers, march off to the swing set, and leave the unchosen behind to pick at their sweaters and wonder what's wrong with them. We have had a lot of trouble with recess this year, but as chief counselor in my daughter's life I have tried to explain how Rachel ticks, hoping to give her a psychological edge over this little toughie who has such a franchise on her heart.

Thus, when she drags herself home from school and confesses to another bad day, I have taken the "excuse me, but is there some compelling reason?" approach in an attempt to give my daughter a partial window into Rachel's soul—all the better to capture it. This is what's known as the "Miracle on 34th Street" approach to evil.

"You know Rachel," I begin. "She is all niceness one day and all crankiness the next. It's her personality. It doesn't have anything to do with you. Maybe she got out on the wrong side of the bed."

My daughter doesn't know about beds and wrong sides thereof. She is only thinking that Rachel teased her about her new boots and said that the boys would like her if she wore them to school again. The fact is however, and I point this out, that Rachel doesn't have a new pair of boots and my daughter does.

"She's probably a little bit jealous," I explain. "And anyway, what's wrong with boys liking you?" What indeed! The next week, Rachel came to school flashing an identical pair of boots. But, as it is with these self-confident, charismatic types, she did not think it necessary to explain her own reversal. Nor did it occur to my daughter, who simply reported the reversal without judgment, to demand an explanation.

The trouble with Rachel is that she marches to a drum that is often difficult to decode. One never knows from one day to the next when those pale eyes will fill with affection or darken with disdain. And looking at my sorrowing daughter, I can't help wondering if she couldn't use a different sort of counseling, where we think less about doping out Rachel's psyche and more about throwing an ice cream party to which we pointedly don't invite Rachel. That would teach her to stop switching around with my daughter's life. Or would it?

Saint Francis and the Cosa Nostra have butted against each other in my thoughts for over a year now, but the other afternoon the sheep got speedily separated from the goats.

Sinking down at the kitchen table, my daughter gave a large sigh, lowered her head into her arms, and began to weep.

"What's the matter?"

"It's Rachel," she sobbed.

"What about her?"

"She said," sobbed my daughter, raising her head just long enough to finish the sentence, "that I have Chinese eyes."

My daughter does indeed have almond-shaped, slightly Chinese-looking eyes. They are beautiful. Every adult who has ever met her thinks so. But

Rachel, with deadly accuracy, had just zeroed in on the one physical attribute that has always been a great source of identity worry for my daughter. Something inside snapped.

"Listen," I said quietly, "you must never tell Rachel this, but you are ten times more beautiful than she'll ever be. You don't know it but I do, and what's more, you are smarter, nicer, and I wouldn't take ten Rachels for one of you. She's mean, selfish, and tries to make herself feel better by making other children feel worse. I even know some grown-ups like that, and you ought to be glad that you aren't that sort of a person."

My daughter gazed solemnly across the table, mentally digesting this unexpected dose of classified information. A short silence ensued.

"But," she asked quietly, "what should I say if Rachel teases me again about my eyes?"

I thought a moment, gave the hip-check to Saint Francis, and told her in a most graphic way what to tell Rachel she could do.

My daughter had never heard me use such a description before, but the look on her face told me she knew exactly what I meant. She smiled broadly, cocked her small head to one side, and said softly, "And then maybe I could tell her (expletive deleted)!"

Dear God, where did she get that one? "No," I replied as evenly as possible, "I think that's going a bit too far."

22.

Perilous Times

Some time ago I read about an experiment in which two laboratory rats from widely divergent backgrounds were thrown into a large vat of water. Rat number one had been raised with a silver spoon in his mouth. His maze was well-lit, there was always enough cheese in the refrigerator, and until he was plucked from his maze altogether, he had always had great faith in what lay around the corner.

But Rat number two had been conditioned to believe that life was a series of cruel frustrations. His maze was full of dead ends, what cheese was available he had to go through hell to get, and half the time he bit into a chunk it was wired for shock. He grew up mean, lean, and justifiably suspicious.

The scientists were curious to know which rat in the vat would drown first—the optimist or the survivor. Within the hour they had their answer. The rat with the rotten life had said, "Nuts to you," and sunk to the bottom, while the rat with the positive attitude paddled around quite a bit longer, under the false illusion that this couldn't possibly be happening to him.

In these financially frightening times, I don't know which rat I identify with most, and it's difficult to take any comfort from an experiment in which both rats died in the end. But I find myself chanting F.D.R.'s "The only thing to fear is fear itself" like a mantra against tomorrow, and some nights I am sleepless with dread. But the next morning, when *The New Yorker* arrives in the mail, I ask myself, "Can someone who still gets *The New Yorker* go broke?"

It doesn't seem possible, with Erica Wilson urging me to come to her Nantucket Needlework Seminar on page 122. Now there's a lady who knows how to turn a brick into a doorstop, something which I like to think I know how to do, too. But sometimes I lose faith. Within this very house there are two people without jobs hanging around the telephone on the odd chance that it might ring for them. Next month it may not ring at all. Along with the last *New Yorker* came a disconnect notice from the telephone company, although they are not quite ready to call me a full-fledged bum yet. At the bottom of their notice was the printed message "It's a pleasure to do business with you." On the final notice they probably say, "Nuts to you," and jerk out the service.

I tend to laugh at disconnect notices and dinnertime calls from MasterCard representatives, because I was raised, like the rat with the positive approach, to believe that the lights might flicker but they would never go out. There was always an alternative to picking up coal from the railroad tracks if only you thought hard enough. And failing a solution, you simply adopted a "Five Little Peppers" attitude toward financial embarrassment and sang songs in the dark. Better yet, sell the songs.

Yet I'm not sure this isn't paddling in the vat under the delusion that the rescue squad is on its way. It makes me uncomfortable to see a pregnant friend delivering telephone books. I don't find it amusing to discover that the woman I planned to hit up for a loan if I got desperate has canceled her newspaper subscription. I can't buy potholders without a guilty conscience, and every time I walk into an expensive children's shoe store, where doctors' kids in alligator shirts are trying to decide between Nikes and Adidases, I wonder whether this is the last time I'll be allowed in the door. When will they find me out and refer me to the sneaker bin at Korvette's?

But a confession is in order. I find the danger exhilarating. Every time I pass a credit card through someone's computer, I feel as if somebody has stamped another "O.K." on my chest. A bunch of daffodils I can't afford enables me to thumb my nose at the cost-of-living index; and at my most perilous financial moments, I find myself buying Le Creuset pots and thousand-year loafers from L. L. Bean, following the instinct to buy something that is more durable than myself. I have come to think that the streets are full of fearful people driving new cars with the windows rolled up, feeling temporarily safe because their transmissions are still under guarantee. Fear drives people apart.

I am not in love with the theory that "poor is more," although I don't know what to say to people who think secondhand mattresses are, ipso facto, full of germs. Many of my best friends are selling their engagement rings, shopping the throwaway bins at the Safeway, and thinking twice before they jump in the car to drive across town for a cup of coffee.

Everyone I know is open at the pockets. My income-tax man plays the piano when he comes over to the house, just to make me feel better. We sing in the semidarkness together. Movies are better than ever, or so I've heard. I half expect to be squeezing the yellow dot in the margarine and making tinfoil balls before we're out of the woods. But the man with the mustache hasn't foreclosed . . . yet. This is the twilight zone. Thank God my father forced me to learn shorthand. I still have my health.

Sing on, little rat. Have faith in what lies around the corner. It may be a life preserver. If all else fails, I will float on my back.

23.

On Hating Piano Lessons

When I was growing up, I conceived of children as being of two kinds: those who took lessons and those who did not. I was the second kind, although I sometimes accompanied my horseback-riding, accordion-playing, baton-twirling friends to their classes and, by osmosis, learned a few things that enabled me to fake an expertise in a crowd. But with one exception I was self-taught, flinging my arms and legs around the living room doing badly executed *tours jetés* to Gilbert and Sullivan records, which allowed me to assume all the parts and, on one occasion, to break my ankle. I did, however, take piano lessons.

Once I discovered the sound that three fingers simultaneously placed on the right keys could produce, I longed so loudly and consistently for piano lessons that my mother began to think maybe I was a genius and she did not want to go to her grave thinking I had become a short-order cook for want of an option. Op-

131

tions, in the long run, are what lessons are all about.

Now I am a parent. I think about giving my children options and lessons, although children don't understand that their once-a-week session with Madame Faustini at the keyboard cancels out their mother's once-a-month visit to "The Magic Scissors." But haircuts play second fiddle to Beethoven if I am financially solvent, and this year my ten-year-old daughter is taking piano lessons—under duress.

My daughter does not like piano lessons. They are too hard. Her teacher, a wild and dedicated woman who drives around in a yellow convertible and annually volunteers to sit on the "Dunk-'Em" chair at the school bazaar, understands about ten-year-old girls who would rather be talking on the telephone, and she always tries to give her pieces to learn that are on the jazzy side. But my daughter, though dutiful, has not been won over by this enlightened approach. Furthermore, she claims, her heart lies with gymnastics, a message I bought last year, along with a leotard which now lies neglected in her bottom bureau drawer.

When she was halfway through gymnastics, her heart began to rove down the hall toward a tap-dancing class that sounded a lot better to her ears. I canceled gymnastics and enrolled her in tap, wanting to stake this small developing plant, my daughter, with the kinds of support that would strengthen and develop her soul.

Unfortunately, her soul turned out to be a shifting, shiftless creature, and her interest in tap dancing waned after the sixth lesson. Suddenly, she saw pottery (which happened to have a class in the same building) as the wave of her future. But tiring of always chasing cultural advantages that were in another room, I decided that what my daughter wanted was immaterial. I wanted her to take piano lessons.

At the beginning, all was well. But when she had gone through the honeymoon period of her first few lessons and realized there was more to it than pasting gold stars in new music books, gymnastics began to appeal to her anew. This time, however, I looked her straight in the eye and said, unflinchingly, "This year it's piano lessons. In fact, next year it's piano lessons, too, unless I can't afford them." It seemed important to let her know that there was no way out.

My daughter thinks I am cruel, that I don't understand her, that I am trying to force her to be something she is not. My daughter is right. I want her, when she is thirty-five or sixty and feeling temporarily low on being, to be able to converse with Mozart, call up Clementi, or have a romp with Rodgers and Hammerstein at *will*, which is what lessons of any kind develop the capacity to use.

This is a difficult wish to communicate to a child who looks at me with "don't make me do it" eyes when I drop her off for a lesson where she must spend another hour forcing her mind and fingers up and down the G and treble clefts. But I have hardened myself to her accusatory looks, and while my daughter has her reasons for complaint, my old heart has its reasons for making her suffer which her heart, being young, cannot fully understand.

There will come a time, I think, as I watch you trudge up the steps to your teacher's house, when your heart will be empty. There will come a time when words, no matter how many or how eloquent, will do you no good at all. There will come a time when no one thing or person can adequately express the soul inside you that needs to be articulated. And then, my gymnastic, tap-dancing daughter, if I have been sufficiently "cruel" to you, you will have music.

But Time divides us at this moment. There are some things one cannot explain to a ten-year-old girl who is only in Book One of piano and life. I must adjust myself to being the mean parent who doesn't understand, and perhaps I don't. Perhaps my daughter *is* a gymnast, or a tap dancer, or the world's number one potter who, when she is grown, will rightly accuse me of having thrown her on the wrong wheel. But in the meantime, in-between time, she is taking piano lessons.

24.

Mr. Olson

In late summer, as all gardeners know, we approach final harvest, or at least most of us do. In my case I am approaching weeds, six-foot-tall stands of lamb's-quarters which have split my cabbage, overrun the bush beans, and caused the garden manager, Mr. Olson, to telephone me frequently to sorrow over my tomatoes, which I keep forgetting to pick. This kind of waste befuddles Mr. Olson who, at seventy-three, has never let a tomato or a Social Security check slip through his fingers. But this morning my weeds caught up with me.

"Thought you'd like to know," said Mr. Olson, with an edge in his voice, "that the Park Service is going to inspect us next week." I could not fail to take his meaning, and putting down the telephone I advanced upon my plot.

The sun was high but not hot, good weeding weather. It had rained heavily the night before. The weeds came up easily, except for the mint, about which I don't feel so "julepy" anymore. Gone today, here tomorrow as far as mint is concerned. It would just as soon suffocate a squash as look at it. But I wasn't trying to project the blame for this wreckage on anything else this morning. Although plowing through the overgrowth, looking for root causes, I was amazed to find that despite my neglect the garden had grown.

One, two, three plump carrots were pulled up. I stumbled on a zucchini that had survived against the odds. Cherry tomatoes, which apparently don't care what's going on around them, lay like Easter Eggs everywhere. I piled the weeds I deserved on my left, the harvest I didn't deserve on my right.

Midway I stopped to pick a handful of zinnias and admire a Monarch butterfly which was hanging with silk-screened wings extended off a marigold. "Is it not," wrote Robinson Jeffers, "by his high superfluousness that we know our God? For to equal a need is natural, animal, mineral. But to fling rainbows over the rain . . ."

I have never wanted to harvest a butterfly. For that matter, I am not keen on harvesting cherry tomatoes either. Gardening tends to raise certain truths and lower others—like why I am here—although if I had to take an entrance exam I would cheerfully lie and say, "For the food."

Mr. Olson, who silently materialized over my weeding body, does not deal in poetry. He sees a tomato and a Mason jar simultaneously. In fact, he sees hundreds of Mason jars lining his basement shelves, and in the event of a nuclear attack I will head for his doorstep and wait for the all clear. He could feed

Boys' Town for a year on what he harvests from his garden.

Mr. Olson is a happy, thrifty man who saves everything except Mrs. Olson, who has a bad back and is not wild about the canning process, and I wonder if she might be just as happy living on junk food in Miami Beach with all worries about botulism behind her.

But Mrs. Olson rarely comes to the garden, except to supervise the potato planting. I would too if I had coaxed fifty seedlings out of one Idaho potato soaked in a pan of water.

"Fifty plants out of one potato!" I exclaimed.

"That's right," said Mr. Olson, "and we had the mother potato for lunch after that."

"How could you," I remonstrated, "after all she's done?"

Mr. Olson's plot and my own adjoin, but our minds don't always, although I don't have one homegrown potato to my name, and Mr. Olson, who cures them on his living room floor under an electric blanket turned on to "medium" overnight, has a million.

As I weeded, Mr. Olson mused, musing being one of the small luxuries of his advanced foresight. ("I'm a mulch man," he declared. "You don't see me breaking my back.")

"Been lots of people who don't pick their things," he remarked. "I try to warn them that their stuff will go to waste, but what can you do?"

"Nothing," I agreed, trying to change the subject by finishing it. "We'll all pay for our neglect at the supermarket, in cash."

"I don't worry about money," said Mr. Olson. "Why, just this week I lost fourteen thousand dollars."

I let that one slip by. Mr. Olson has trapped me before on the subject. His favorite saying is "It's not the high cost of living, it's the cost of living high."

Mr. Olson has a fund of aphorisms that would outdo Alexis de Tocqueville, although if de Tocqueville had met anyone like Mr. Olson when he was visiting America, he would have been thoroughly confused. Mr. Olson looks like a farmer, but he has made his fortune in shopping malls, dance studios, and land, but not for land's sake. He just cheerfully sold off 500 lush acres for a commercial airport, and during the Depression he ran a grocery store, showing an instinct for being on the right side of the counter. On the other hand, he did just lose $14,000. I decided to ask him how.

"I sold some stock at nine and three quarters, which rose to thirteen by the end of the week."

"What did you buy it at?" I pursued, after giving my brain the five minutes it needed to come up with this astute followup question.

"Two and a half," he conceded. Trapped again.

On the strengths of these kinds of "losses," Mr. Olson drives a fishtail Oldsmobile with a gold-carpeted trunk that lights up like a refrigerator at night to reveal a stack of Gideon Bibles which he distributes to prisoners at the local penitentiary. The prison offers a pretty good lunch, which Mr. Olson tries to stay over for when he can. They also throw away plastic buckets at the jail, "good, durable ones," which Mr. Olson collects and puts under his downspouts to reduce his water bill every year.

"I call it my miracle water," he said. I call Mr. Olson a miracle.

At the end of my weeding, I tried to carry the harvest I did not deserve back home. No bag, no foresight. Loading the cherry tomatoes into the front of my skirt, I walked gingerly back to the car. Easing up to the open window, I tried to dump the contents into the seat. It didn't work. Three dozen cherry tomatoes spilled out of my skirt and began to roll like jack balls down the hill.

I tried to head them off at the pass, but they were too quick for me. They bounced, zigzagged, and danced independently down the road, my harvest on the lam.

I was glad that Mr. Olson was not there to witness this final failure, but as I watched the runaway crop roll cheerfully out of control I canned the only thing I had left—chagrin.

25.

The Price of Love

For the past several years I have been a gardener, and that first spring I approached the soil with inexperience, trepidation, and a bag full of seeds, which I planted with trembling fingers, unsure as to whether anything I planted would actually grow. But things did and to my eyes each marigold head was a wonder, each cucumber blossom a miracle; and as I sat in the midst of an aromatic bower of tomato plants which only weeks before had been mere slips in cardboard containers, I was filled with exaltation, poetry, and a sweet sense of power that I had never experienced before. In retrospect, that was my honeymoon phase in the garden—the year I fell in love with the idea. But the second year was a second story, less poetic but more instructive than the first.

Knowing it all, I approached the same plot of ground with overconfidence. I did not take the time to crumble lovingly each clod of soil in my fingers, with the respect it deserved, reminding me that the earth will not be trifled with, and that summer my garden was passable, but not the glistening cornucopia other gardeners passed by for inspiration. And the third season my garden was a mockery of weeds, perishing from my lack of commitment, which is the true test of love once the bloom is off the rose.

This year I will approach the soil with new humility, having learned that anything less than humility does not serve the gardener well. And, like many others, I have come to see that the correlation between gardening and life is rather exact. Humility, replaced by pride, replaced by a new humility: We are raised up only to be lowered, like fresh leaves that dissolve into mulch in order to nourish a new crop of greenery, ensuring that youth will always be served in the end. Which reminds me of Colleen.

She was as young as her name. There was a round and rosy completeness to her that was not the result of experience as much as having just arrived, full-blown, on the threshold where everything experiential is about to begin, and the moment she walked through the front door, I felt like a complex bed of mulch in the presence of a simple string-bean kernel. Of course, mulch has its memories. But as I cast back to my twenty-first year of life, Colleen did not remind me very much of myself.

She wore a matching hat, scarf, and mittens, bespeaking an organizational ability I did not possess at her age. She had brought her own pressure cooker. I did not haul pressure cookers around at twenty-one, I hauled angst and the sneaking feeling that the God of my childhood was going to be insufficient to my adult years. Then, too, she was shy, an emotion I admire but is contrary to my nature. Her brown eyes were slightly at odds with her smile, as if she were trying to bring the two together to make a solid statement and not quite succeeding.

But she radiated an innocence I remembered having. Clutching her suitcase full of cardigan sweaters and pink letter paper, she was shot through with it, like a peach in the sunlight. "How pretty she is," I thought, a statement I used to invert and ask of myself as I traveled back and forth on the commuter train between college and New York.

The train window, when we plunged into tunnels, was a dark mirror which gave back a face that was pretty enough, although that was not my first concern. Was that face the face of someone going crazy? At twenty-one the first cracks in my consciousness were painfully acute to me, and on the train, through a glass darkly, I would gaze into my own eyes and try to ascertain whether to the casual observer I appeared as mentally unstable as I knew myself to be.

This was not Colleen's problem. What she knew of her own soul seemed to refresh her at the source, and as she stood in the front hall pulling off her mittens, she exuded a Scotch-plaid orderliness and tranquillity that was neither off-putting nor enviable given her age. Innocence is a hard handicap. It takes one many years to replace it with something slightly more durable, like wisdom, and, God knows, wisdom is only a sometime thing. But Colleen glowed with innocence so enthusiastically, like a new candle with a fresh wick, that one was effortlessly drawn to her with a mixture of admiration and awe.

"This is Colleen," I said, introducing her to my lawyer, who had dropped by to discuss some of the less innocent aspects of my life.

"Sure 'n' how could she be called anything else," he

had exclaimed, and Colleen laughed. Her Irishness advanced her like the freckles on her nose, and in another age she might have been a milkmaid or, laced up in a bodice, serving ale to gentlemen in a Galway pub.

But this was the 1980's. Colleen was a fledgling career girl, coming to live here as a part-time bottle washer and babysitter in the evening, while pursuing her larger destiny downtown during the day. Our house was a way station, neither complete independence nor her small town, fifty miles away, full of shampoo-grabbing younger sisters whom Colleen had just left behind.

Her plans, prior to unpacking her suitcase, had already been well laid out in advance, which was how Colleen always advanced her life. Before she had been here twenty-four hours, she was efficiently advancing mine. Menus were organized. The refrigerator was cleaned. She tore out recipes to put on the bulletin board, and her own schedule, within three days, was entirely fixed. Colleen thrived on order, viewing each day as a load of laundry to be sorted, washed, and put away before it got the jump on a person. But she was not averse to surprise developments. For someone with such a penchant for swept surfaces, Colleen loved the unexpected, if it was pleasant, like the delivery of new kitchen cabinets from Sears.

But Colleen, unbeknownst to herself, was in for a development that took both of us by surprise. In fact, the development had already taken place, like a seed silently planted which had already begun to extend its roots below the soil. In my ignorance I spent the first several weeks fussing over Colleen's entry into a larger, more art-galleried world. I should have taken the phone off the hook instead.

His name was David. Only a week before Colleen's

arrival, he had met her at her parents' house. Being smart, provident, and possessed of a keen eye, he had taken one look at Colleen and decided that her stay in this house and this city would be as brief and unsatisfactory as he could make it—from fifty miles away, after eleven in the evening, when the telephone rates went down.

I do not blame David. He only saw what anyone could see—that despite Colleen's assets, which might ultimately serve her well as board chairman of General Mills, her parallel destiny was to make some abjectly grateful man extremely happy. David saw that abjectly grateful man as himself.

Of course, he had nothing against art galleries, evening courses in advanced Italian, or Colleen's desire to dip her wings into the wider world. But he was no fool. There was competition he couldn't sideswipe at a distance, a lot of handsome Porsche-driving devils in turtleneck sweaters, who worked as real-estate appraisers, and would know, as did David, a good thing when they saw it.

Or so I imagine his line of reasoning to have been. I only met David twice during the time Colleen was here, and he was a clear-eyed, eminently likable person who knew a great deal about cars and life, knowledge which eludes me still. But most of the time, David was an unheard voice at one end of many telephone conversations that punctuated the late evenings after the children were asleep. Before 11 P.M. Colleen lived her life according to her original plan. But after 11 P.M. it suffered nightly disorganizational raids.

As the weeks went by and it became increasingly difficult to imagine how I had ever managed to live without Colleen in the first place, her face began to lose some of its round, rosy certitude. She took to sighing, acting distracted, spending time in her room, at odds with her usual even-tempered self. She was, I realized, struggling hard with an unfamiliar conflict that would not resolve itself. One evening she came down into the kitchen to think through the conflict out loud.

Sitting at the kitchen table, her life efficiently cinched around her waist like the sash of her terry-cloth bathrobe, she ticked off reasons for staying here. On the one hand, she hardly knew David. She had a commitment to me. She had just accepted a new job. She liked that job. She wanted to experience a lot of things. There were more reasons than fingers to think that packing up her suitcase and moving back home to be near David was not a very sensible idea. Colleen always liked to be sensible. But on the other hand, all of her fingers blurred together.

"I don't know," she said. "Always before, boys have liked me, but I have never really thought that I could feel the same way toward them. But David, he . . ." Her head felt muddled, pleasantly so. Thinking at all was like trying to get to Oz through a field of opium poppies.

Colleen was at a crossroads. I knew it. She knew it. And as I sat across the kitchen table, wearing my own life like an interesting but raveled evening dress, I tried to organize my own thoughts.

The first exercise I had to perform in order to purify my intentions was mentally to pry my fingers off Colleen's life. "Easy come, easy go," I thought. "Just because Colleen fills the air with hyacinths, loves to cook, and thinks my children are interesting, conversational human beings, just because she has made this house over in an image I approve of much more than my own, these are not reasons to make her feel guilty for wanting to leave."

Having spoken strictly with myself, I looked across the table at Colleen and thought about her dilemma anew.

"You are very young," I said.

Colleen accepted this statement humbly. "I know," she conceded. Age was not her strong suit.

"I wish," I added, "when I had been your age that I had spent a little time on my own."

"I'm not afraid of being alone," said Colleen, and I had to admit that she had already done more at twenty-one than I would have dreamed of doing. Two unaccompanied trips to Europe, traveling around the Continent, learning French and Italian en route. No, Colleen was not blackmailed by fear of empty spaces. But she did have her dreams, awfully similar to my own at her age, when I viewed my future as a giant dime store full of wicker baskets, pillows, and gingham material waiting to be made up into curtains for the kitchen of my ultimate house. I knew the power of these images. They transcended ideology or right-thinking articles by women who wielded No. 2 pencils and wore suits by Cardin.

"Is there any reason why you can't have your cake and eat it too?" I asked, knowing in my heart that I had never pulled that trick off myself. "Couldn't you stay here, keep your job, and see David on weekends? That way you could get to know each other slowly and would know if he was the one for you or not."

That seemed reasonable to Colleen, but her face remained in conflict. "I don't know," she murmured. "It just doesn't seem like that would be possible . . ." Her voice trailed off apologetically, as if the only person she could continue the discussion with was herself.

"Look, Colleen," I continued. "Nobody can ever give anyone else advice, and stop me if this sounds too commercially minded. But it seems to me that if you want to go back and get your teaching degree next year, you could stay here until June, save the tuition money you need, and then when you left, you wouldn't have that to worry about. The money would be right there."

"I've never worried about money," said Colleen softly, unwittingly driving a shaft into the middle of one value from which I, too, have always felt quite detached. "Look at the lilies of the field," I used to instruct myself when money lowered its head in my bank account. No, I never worried about money either, until I began to worry about it. But here was Colleen, sitting straight as a lily in an opposite chair, self-confidently proclaiming her faith in the providence which, so far, had always clothed her and I had no doubt always would. She shamed me.

"You're right," I countered. "Money should never be the most important factor in a life decision. But," I added, feeling old and tired and worried about rain gutters that needed replacing, "money does count for something, and I wish that when I was your age, before I had gotten married, that I had saved a little."

"Oh, I'm not thinking about getting married," said Colleen, although in the rosy light of the wicker lamp that hung over the table, Colleen looked like a Dutch master's rendering of a young girl whose entire being was wrapped up in anticipation of something quite similar to that Sacrament.

I never found it possible to look at Colleen without thinking the same thing, that she was so pretty, so pink-cheeked, so golden, with her long hair curling naturally down the planes of both cheeks. But as I looked at her under the lamplight, I knew that truth had to be served, and gathering up all my past mistakes, present understandings, and least perishable bits of wisdom, I embarked upon a monologue, neither harsh nor sentimental, neither too plain nor too obscure.

I have come to think that women give advice to their younger sisters for one reason: in expiation for their own lives, which they hold like lamps above the heads of their successors, to warn them of the chuckholes and blind alleys that might lie ahead. Or perhaps we are like aging tennis pros. I was trying to show Colleen how to position her hand on the tennis racket, all the better to swing.

First, I took up the theme of independence, which I knit through the themes of freedom, responsibility, and commitment to oneself before taking on anyone else. The dropped stitches in my life became the holes which I held up for her inspection. But all these themes seemed to cast more shadow than light. Finally, I stopped talking, suddenly tired of the droning, pedantic sound of my own voice.

"I see what you're saying," said Colleen, who had listened with her brown eyes wide open, like the stuck shutter of a camera, determined to expose her mind to as much light as she could bear. "I guess I should think about these things," she added. "Everything you say makes sense. But all I can say is that I've never felt this way about anybody before. And it seems to me that if you do feel this way for the first time that you ought to take that seriously, too."

Her voice trailed off and suddenly, in the silence, I was smitten with remorse. There was something I had come perilously close to forgetting, and to forget it altogether would have been to be irretrievably old, beyond recall.

One of the judgmental clichés currently floating around is the statement "well (sigh), he (or she) just isn't *there,* yet." The implication is, of course, that we already are there, while the person under discussion is still evolving toward the superior breadth of understanding we already possess. Perhaps. Perhaps not.

So many superior understandings in my possession have crumbled under second scrutiny that I wonder whether anyone has the right to judge who is ahead of whom, anymore than one can rank fir trees ahead of rose buds, or herb tea ahead of beer. Destinies differ. We are each wrapped within separate clockworks, proceeding through time at our own speed—unless we "fall in love."

Love stops the clock. Two sets of minute hands are synchronized and the center of the universe is right here in this pizza parlor where two people are silently rejoicing over the miraculous paradox of being alone together in the same place at the same time. When we are in love, we are in a time warp, and the power and poetry of the experience is—how could I have forgotten this?—full of a sharp joy that organizes the universe around the heart.

I looked at Colleen, remembering many things she did not know about me. Then I remembered my garden. Last spring I planted string beans. Several weeks later they began to sprout through the soil, tiny, pale-green leaves still attached to the seeds themselves which had burst their containers and sent the first shoots upward. String beans are born in extreme humility. Each shoot presents itself bowed over, in a kind of breech-birth position, before it finally releases itself from the seed pod and stands straight up.

Bowed over in the lamplight, Colleen reminded me of a newborn string bean, struggling to free herself from the mother pod, instinctively pulling away from the dark earth toward the light.

"Colleen," I began.

She looked up, expecting me to present yet another millstone that I wanted to try around her neck for size.

"I want you to forget everything I have just said."

"What do you mean?" she asked.

"Just what I said," I answered. "Forget it all."

"Why?" she persisted. "Don't you believe what you've been saying?"

"Yes," I answered. "But you're in love, Colleen. You may not know it yet, but that's just what you are. There's nothing like it, it's wonderful. And," I added, "it's about time."

Colleen straightened up her head and smiled, a wide, relieved smile, as if, released from her obligations to the mother pod, she could spread her leaves a little and tackle the sun head on.

Which is just what she did and I have missed her every day since she left. To me, it seems like the right decision, or an inspired wrong one. When you're in love, all the opposites join up together. But if angels float over pizza parlors, I imagine they are equally divided between those who rejoice and those who weep. One doesn't have to be an angel to know that time always moves on.

26.

Time and a River

There was a time when all of time lay ahead of me. I don't exactly remember what I did with this asset except look at it and wonder how I could advance the clock a little in order to get on with real life. But real life held its hazards.

A part of me hung back, not wanting to put my life on the line unless I knew that the line was going to hold. Time was a river, bright with possibilities. But it was also a muscular current that could bear me unsympathetically right over Niagara Falls if I wasn't careful, which I tried very hard to be.

Child time is both an anchor and an irresistible force that can wash you over the edge, and the other afternoon, when my youngest son was invited to go on a real river in a real boat, I remembered why, although not all at once.

At first, he was thrilled. But within seconds he was having second thoughts.

"What about the rapids?" he asked.

"There won't be any," I reassured him. "The river is at its lowest at this time of year."

"Suppose the boat cracks in two?" he asked.

"It won't crack in two," I answered. "Canoes are very strong."

"I wish it were a kayak. In a kayak you're more covered up."

A discussion on the safety of canoes versus kayaks ensued, followed by a discussion of just how deep the water was at this time of year, and did wood (as in shards of the canoe which had already split in his imagination) float? I began to feel a certain amount of exasperation. Given two ways to spend a Saturday, loafing around the playground or slicing through the waters like an Indian in autumn, my son was opting for inertia. He rarely chose that course.

This is the child who last week was discovered begging with his best friend, "Dirt II" (my son is "Dirt I" in the A.D.A., or "All Dirt Association"), outside the local drugstore.

"If you ever do that again, I'll break your neck," said his older brother, who has his reputation to consider.

"Begging!" I exclaimed. "What did you say?"

"I told people I needed money because my father had been killed and my mother had committed suicide."

"Did you have any luck?" I asked, feeling grateful that neither one of his parents had succumbed to this drama.

"Not as much as last week," he conceded.

"Last week!" I shouted. "How long has this been going on?"

"That time I pretended to be blind. Billy [Dirt II]

led me around by his hand and said, 'Arms for the poor!' "

I privately filed away "arms for the poor" as being an improvement on the original expression, and publicly ruled out any future begging expeditions until such time as we were really hard up. The child has chutzpah, I thought, although playing at life and being directly involved in it were obviously two different things.

The subject of the river ride was not over. The adult continued to push for a good time while the child continued to speak from the depths of Tom Sawyer's cave, trying to explain something that refused to come out in so many words. Namely, that he was petrified. We were canoes passing in the night, the mother prattling on about a fun-filled afternoon on the water, the son trying to cut through her Kiwanis Club optimism to plead for his survival.

"I wouldn't know what to do if there was a thunderstorm," he whispered. "I mean with lightning . . ." Suddenly, the landscape in his mind lit up in mine.

I saw him as he saw himself, white-faced and puny in the middle of a rolling current, electrified by panic, about to be folded into a death-dealing river that would sweep him into a gorge, a sewer pipe, or some other maw from which he would never return. I was terrified on his behalf. Then something occurred to me.

"Do you remember," I said, "the other day when we were talking about Lincoln and how he freed the slaves?"

He nodded, unsure as to why we were discussing social studies just now. "Well," I continued, "you told me that if you had been a slave you would have run away in order to be free."

He nodded again. I felt I was gaining on him in my big, powered-by-reason boat.

"There is more than one way to be a slave," I explained. "If you are a slave to your fears, you aren't free to do what you really want—like going on a boat ride."

He understood. He decided, in the wake of my flawless logic, that he would go on the boat ride after all. But between afternoon and evening the connection between Lincoln and canoes dissolved in his mind.

"I've thought it over," he said, flopping on the sofa, "and I still don't want to go."

"Why not?" I asked.

"I don't know," he admitted, "but deep down in my bones I just think it's going to be a disaster."

It was time to give up. Perhaps he knew something I didn't know and tomorrow I would read about it in the newspapers.

"The thing is," he continued, "I just don't like to do things unless I know what's going to happen."

"Ah," I said. "So you want to make sure everything will be all right before you start out."

"Yeah," he said. "I want to know things for sure, like about God, and whether I'm going to get sick, or get cancer or . . . I want to know everything that's going to happen to me."

"Well," I answered, knowing that I didn't have an answer that would relieve him of the necessity of finding this out for himself, "part of growing up is learning how to live with not knowing. After a while it doesn't seem so bad. In fact, you begin to wonder whether it isn't better not to know."

He looked at me, trying to understand what in the world I had just said. It didn't make much sense to someone nine years old whose entire life still remained to be seen.

"You're lucky," he said, propping his head up on one hand as he gazed at me from the sofa.

"Lucky?" I queried. "Why?"

"Because you're a grown-up," he answered solemnly. "You've already made it through."